Petite Pizzazz

♥ Other books available from Chilton:

Robbie Fanning, Series Editor

Creative Machine Arts Series

Claire Shaeffer's Fabric Sewing Guide

The Complete Book of Machine Embroidery, by Robbie and Tony Fanning

Creative Nurseries Illustrated, by Debra Terry and Juli Plooster

Creative Serging Illustrated, by Pati Palmer, Gail Brown, and Sue Green

Distinctive Gifts and Crafts, by Naomi Baker and Tammy Young

The Expectant Mother's Wardrobe Planner, by Rebecca Dumlao

The Fabric Lover's Scrapbook, by Margaret Dittman

Friendship Quilts by Hand and Machine, by Carolyn Vosburg Hall

Innovative Serging, by Gail Brown and Tammy Young

Innovative Sewing, by Gail Brown and Tammy Young

Know Your Bernina, second ed., by Jackie Dodson

Know Your Brother, by Jackie Dodson with Jane Warnick

Know Your Elna, by Jackie Dodson with Carol Ahles

Know Your New Home, by Jackie Dodson with Judi Cull and Vicki Lynn Hastings

Know Your Pfaff, by Jackie Dodson with Audrey Griese

Know Your Sewing Machine, by Jackie Dodson

Know Your Simplicity, by Jackie Dodson with Jane Warnick

Know Your Singer, by Jackie Dodson

Know Your Viking, by Jackie Dodson with Jan Saunders

Know Your White, by Jackie Dodson with Jan Saunders

Owner's Guide to Sewing Machines, Sergers, and Knitting Machines, by Gale Grigg Hazen

Sew, Serge, Press, by Jan Saunders

Sewing and Collecting Vintage Fashions, by Eileen MacIntosh

Simply Serge Any Fabric, by Naomi Baker and Tammy Young

Contemporary Quilting Series

Fast Patch, by Anita Hallock

Speed-Cut Quilts, by Donna Poster

(watch for more books)

Petite Pizzazz

Barb Griffin

Creative Machine Arts Series

Chilton Book Company
Radnor, Pennyslvania

Published in Radnor, Pennsylvania 19089, by Chilton Book Company

The following projects in this book first appeared in "Needle & Craft" Magazine: Bear Necessities Boutique and Buttons 'n Bows Painted Shoes

Designed by Martha Vercoutere
Cover Design by Kevin Culver
Cover photos by Lee Phillips
Photographs by Lee Phillips and Bill Scherer
Illustrations by Barb Griffin
Models: Kendal and Megan Dazey

Manufactured in the United States of America

Library of Congress Cataloging-in-Publication Data

Griffin, Barb
    Petite pizzazz / Barb Griffin.
        p. cm.—(Creative machine arts)
    ISBN 0-8019-7992-7
    1. Children's clothing. 2. Machine sewing. I. Title. II. Series: Creative machine arts series.
TT635.G75 1990   89-45963
646.4'06—dc20   CIP
                       r89

1 2 3 4 5 6 7 8 9 0   9 8 7 6 5 4 3 2 1 0

With love
to my brother, Jim Griffin,
for always believing in me,
and
to the keys of my heart,
Jonathon and Jamie

Contents

Foreword

Glance at Barb Griffin's imaginative ideas and you'll instantly understand why her social calendar reflects so many baby shower invitations. Generous doses of charm and whimsy make her designs a treat to receive. And they are just as much fun to create.

I am lucky enough to have known Barb even before she was famous, back when her designs were exclusives for her own toddlers, Jon and Jamie. The status-y kids' shops near our homes were full of adorable outfits and accessories, but with sticker-shock price tags. Luckily, Barb has an unfailing knack for analyzing exactly what makes a designer outfit special, then finding a way to duplicate all the pizzazz—and for pennies on the dollar.

So for years, I have shamelessly copied Barb idea after Barb idea...and occasionally commissioned a "Barb original"...for family and special friends.

These days Jon and Jamie are college-bound. But thank goodness Barb never outgrew her love of designing for little people. Now that I have finally joined the baby brigade myself, I am delighted to have this whole reference of her creative tips, techniques, and textile artistry to enhance my sewing for twin daughters.

Barb says that dressing a child in an outfit you made is like giving a hug they can wear all day. Thanks to **Petite Pizzazz,** we can give those special hugs to all the precious little people in our lives...and have a good time doing it, too.

♥ **Nancy Nix-Rice**
Baby Lock Product Manager

Preface

Since the time I was married and started a family in 1970, I have always known someone—friend, neighbor, or family member—who was expecting a baby or who had a young tot. My babies are now teenagers, yet that fact hasn't hampered my love of sewing for little ones. I admit that I adore babies, and sewing for babies is one way I continue to nurture that love. With three baby shower invitations on my calendar as I write, my love of sewing tiny finery is able to flourish.

Society has changed a great deal since I was a young mother. Working mothers now outnumber at-home moms by four to one. More discretionary income is available to be spent on babies and toddlers. But the more things change, the more they stay the same. Career women have heard their biological clocks ticking and are answering the call. Original families have broken up for a number of reasons, and people are remarrying and starting families anew. Babies are everywhere! Yes, time is at a premium for working moms—as for all mothers. They are more likely to stitch up garments as a creative outlet than to save money. Whatever the reason, I find the gentle stitchers who create garments and accessories for newborns and toddlers are sewing out of love.

Petite Pizzazz shows you how to put that extra zing into your children's wear with ideas to wrap around your babies all year. Starting with an easy-to-sew layette that has all the style of carriage-trade boutiques, you can welcome baby with a wealth of goodies. Accessories punched with pizzazz make wonderful shower presents.

One thing you can depend on babies to do is grow. Once your child crawls and toddles, he'll be ready for another wardrobe that allows for plenty of movement mixed with style. You'll see how to make outstanding garments that will garner compliments from friends and family alike, along with quick-stitch projects that begin with a purchased garment and add designer detailing.

This book features:

♥ Projects that incorporate purchased items you embellish.

♥ Appliqué designs to add to a garment you sew from a pattern.

♥ Complete patterns for small projects and accessories.

So unleash your creative energies and enjoy the sense of design discovery you'll feel making a baby gift or two. It's like having only one potato chip: you're well satisfied when you're munching, but soon you'll be hungry to stitch again. Happy sewing!

Acknowledgments

No book just happens, and this one had more than its fair share of helping hands and hearts. Special thanks to Robbie Fanning, for her continual support; Kathy Conover and Allison Dodge, the best editors I could ever hope for; and Penny Quint, for being the special friend I could call at all hours for words of encouragement.

And a promise to my children, who ate endless microwave meals, that I won't say the words "Not now, I have a deadline"—well, for at least three months.

Special thanks to these manufacturers for their generous help and wonderful products:

Aleene of Aleene's Division of Artis, Inc.

Almeda Colby of Fibre Crafts, Inc.

Evie Ashworth of Hoffman California Fabrics

Lynita B. Haber of JHB International, Inc.

Ellie Schneider of C. M. Offray and Sons, Inc.

Tulip Paints, Tulip Productions, a Division of Polymerics, Inc.

Introduction

♥ An Insider's Guide to Designer Detailing

Every now and then, I get restless. One of my prescriptions for the blahs, blues, or doldrums is to hop in the car and do a little window shopping. My favorite haunts are exclusive lace and linen shops, children's wear boutiques, and special fabric stores. The crisp designer qualities found in select boutiques make my heart sing. Especially when browsing among baby boutiques, I long to create heirloom quality garments and accessories that say "This baby is to the manor born."

While my budget may not allow me to buy a trunkload of exclusive layette treasures, the items can be studied and their styles copied. What makes the garments so very special? The styles are often classic in design with quality trims. Appliqué, piping, exquisite lace—these details all say quality. Is the garment monogrammed or personalized? By breaking the garment into categories of style, color, appliqué, and trim, it's easy to see how simply the pieces make the whole.

One of my favorite projects is to take an inexpensive item and dress it up. You can start with something as simple as a bib. Using a simple fingertip towel purchased at a linen outlet shop, you cut a 5-1/2" circle for the baby's head and finish with either bias tape or knit ribbing. Add a bright appliqué and a special loop that attaches a teething toy: **instant pizzazz** (Figure I-1). You can tuck a squeaker under the appliqué of a little piggy or make bibs for each day of the week. The result is the equivalent of $10 to $15 bibs shown in popular mail-order catalogs.

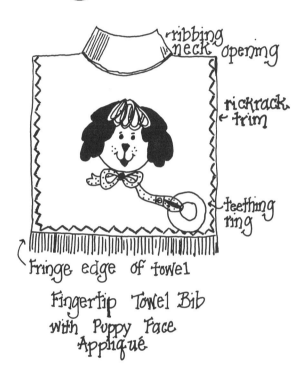

Fig. I-1

To give you an example, let's break down the design elements of the bunting in the Baby Rosebud Boutique in Chapter 1 (Figure 1-17). The materials used for this project totaled $9.75: $5.00 for quilted knit fabric, $1.25 for zipper, $ .50 for flat eyelet lace trim, $ .25 for white ribbing remnant, $ .10 for invisible elastic hood casing, and $2.65 for ribbons. The finished product is a delightful garment that would retail for $50 to $75.

What are the designer elements of this bunting?

♥ Basic garment has simple classic lines.

♥ Fabric is quilted knit in tiny floral print with timeless appeal.

♥ Ribbon roses continue floral print design.

♥ Multi-ribbon bow with streamers under roses matches print hues perfectly.

♥ Top quality flat eyelet lace trims hood.

♥ Quilted design is matched at all seams, including zipper insert.

♥ All seams have finished edges—either overcast or encased with knit bias binding in complementary print.

Nothing here is difficult to assemble, trim, or stitch—yet all details add up to a charming designer-look bunting that would be a welcome addition to a baby's wardrobe.

Repeat this exercise with clothing and accessories you see while shopping or browsing through catalogs. Ask yourself what makes the item special, and make notes if that helps you. Watch for the special trims, ribbons, snaps, or buttons the designers used. Those bits and pieces can transform an item from simple to snazzy.

Once you have begun sewing for a cherished bundle of love, the savings will be overshadowed by the creative joy you experience. Use this book as a jumping-off point. Choose your own theme for a season. Sports, toys, gardening, airplanes, or model cars might hold special appeal to you. Simple cookie-cutter shapes are easily transposed to appliqué. Coloring books are wonderful sources for easy-to-use ideas. The possibilities are limitless.

Before you begin any of the projects, please review the following general how-to section. It will give you a basic understanding of techniques used and will explain materials needed. Please also read complete instructions for each design project before cutting into fabrics, as there may be exceptions to these general instructions.

Commercial pattern companies offer several patterns for making layettes and have whole sections devoted to children's wear. But for the unusual, there are also more and more wonderful alternative companies that offer exquisite patterns: from an heirloom-quality christening gown, to classic designs featuring smocking inserts and quality appliqué, to exclusive designs that rival designer-name creations. At the end of the book a resource list of these companies is included for you along with tested mail-order sources for high-quality knits, notions, and trims.

♥ *Planning the Wardrobe*

Babies and toddlers are very special people, and their clothes should be equally special. Yet tots sparkle naturally; they look and feel best in simple designs. To begin, look for a versatile pattern that follows simple lines with few pieces. You can make one pattern serve several purposes, or combine patterns to make a whole mix-and-match wardrobe. Using different fabrics and trims, and slightly altering the patterns, you can make clothes for every season and every occasion. If you coordinate garments, they will be more versatile,

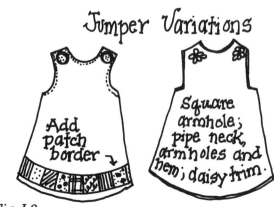
Jumper Variations

Add patch border

Square armhole; pipe neck, armholes and hem; daisy trim.

Fig. I-2

creating a different look for each ensemble. Select colors and fabrics that can be worn year-round. By coordinating colors and detailing, you can achieve a custom look.

Classic button-shoulder garments such as a dress/jumper or jumpsuit look adorable on any child, and because of their simplicity, are easy and fun to decorate. Styles can be cut long or short, with variations such as ruffles added to armholes, decorative waistline casings, zipper placement, knickers with elastic cuffs, or long-lined cuffs for pants (Figure I-2).

♥ *Choosing a Pattern*

I think of children as "miniatures in motion." A baby squirms and twists; toddlers crawl, roll, and tumble; and youngsters are a study in hop, skip, and jump techniques. Their clothing must be able to move with them. When choosing a pattern size, rely on the child's measurements, **not the child's age.** Next, compare your pattern with one of the child's favorite garments to check the fit of the garment you plan to sew. Make changes, adjusting as necessary, for width and/or length on the main pattern.

Some purchased patterns are cut wider than ready-to-wear. Also, some patterns for shirts and tops in small sizes tend to be shorter than ready-to-wear; so measure carefully and adjust accordingly. Because the waist measurement on toddlers, girls, and boys changes less than chest, hip, or length measurements, you may wish to reduce your pattern at the waistline on items with a fitted waist. After altering your pattern as needed, plan to use it as a **master pattern.** Trace patterns from your master, incorporating any design changes you wish to add. **The best method to follow is to measure, adjust, trace, and then cut.** By coordinating fabrics and notions, you can save time by sewing several items using the same pattern.

If you are totally in the dark about infant/toddler ready-to-wear sizes, here are a few tips. On average, babies will triple their birth weight by their first birthday. Sizing for baby clothes can be misleading as the sizes refer to age rather than weight or height. Always choose weight over age guidelines.

Age	Weight Range	Best RTW Size
up to 3 months	up to 10 lbs.	6 months size
3 – 6 months	up to 14 lbs.	12 months size
6 – 9 months	up to 18 lbs.	18 months size
12 months	up to 24 lbs.	24 months size
18 months	up to 28 lbs.	2T (toddler)
24 months	up to 34 lbs.	3T (toddler)

I can't stress this point enough: commercial patterns do not have the same fit as ready-to-wear. So take time to compare well-fitting ready-to-wear to your pattern and adjust accordingly. It's very discouraging to spend valuable time, effort, and money on a garment that won't fit properly.

♥ Appliqué and Quilting Techniques

Don't underestimate the importance of making careful and accurate patterns. Most of the patterns in this book are full-size, ready for you to trace. When you begin a project, check the pattern and directions for seam allowances. Always include all lines, placement details, and labeling when tracing the patterns from this book. This will save you time and headaches later.

Machine appliqué designs are cut on pattern outlines without seam or hem allowance. If you plan to hand appliqué, add a 1/4" seam allowance around the perimeter of each appliqué piece before cutting. For greater durability, patterns that will be used several times can be glued to lightweight cardboard or plastic before they are cut out.

Another alternative to tracing patterns is to photocopy them. Check first to be sure that the reproduction of your copier is accurate. If you need designs reduced or enlarged to fit the size you are making, a photocopy shop can help you for a reasonable charge. Keep in mind the copyright laws: patterns are for personal sewing only. You may use the patterns to make items for family and friends, but projects are not to be manufactured in quantity for resale using these designs.

Appliqué consists of shapes cut from one piece of fabric and applied to another. The shapes, sizes, and colors you choose become the appliqué picture. Traditionally, appliqué was stitched by hand, but machine appliqué is recommended for children's wear because of its durability. It can withstand a great deal of wear and tear.

Appliqué techniques are the same whether you are making a garment or enhancing a purchased one. However, if you are making the garment, it is easier to appliqué individual pieces before assembling the garment.

After you have chosen the project, traced or copied the pattern, and selected your fabrics, back all fabrics to be used for appliqué with lightweight fusible interfacing. I always use a piece of tissue paper between the interfacing and my iron: the fusing material can sometimes melt through, causing a sticky residue on your iron. The tissue paper barrier is the perfect solution, allowing you to see through to the areas you are fusing.

Position and pin pieces according to pattern placement guides. The more I appliqué, the more I have found that placing a little snip of fusible webbing under a piece helps to secure it, eliminating the need for pinning. If you prefer backing all pieces with a fusible webbing such as Stitch Witchery or Aleene's Magic Web, using a glue stick, or pinning your pieces in place, that's fine too. Use the technique that works best for you.

Machine Appliqué

The satin stitch used for appliqué can be sewn by any zigzag sewing machine. It is the zigzag stitch, with stitches placed so close together that they form a thick solid line, with approximately 20 stitches per inch, outlining each appliqué piece.

If machine appliqué is new to you, there are a few quick and easy ways to master this technique. Start by cutting hearts and stars from felt and appliquéing them to a closely woven practice piece, such as poplin or Trigger. Because felt does not fray, it is a good starter fabric. The curves, points, and straight lines of these shapes will give you the variety needed to master appliquéing any shape. Practice pivoting at corners and curves until you are satisfied with the results (Figure I-3). Your lines may wiggle

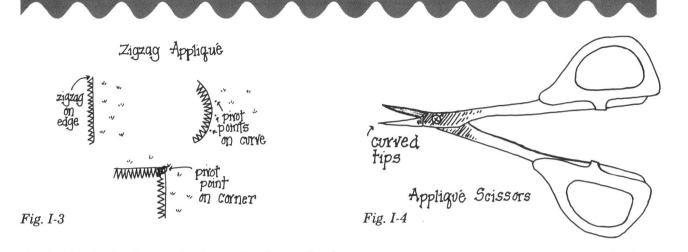

Zigzag Appliqué

zigzag on edge

pivot points on curve

pivot point on corner

Fig. I-3

curved tips

Appliqué Scissors

Fig. I-4

a little at first, but with practice, you will improve quickly.

Next, practice appliquéing hearts and stars cut out of mini-dot, solid, or calico scraps you have on hand. Once again, be sure to back these pieces with lightweight fusible interfacing for a better finished look.

Slightly loosen the upper tension of your sewing machine until you can see the upper thread on the underside of your sample appliqué scrap. This way, the bobbin thread will always be hidden so you won't need to change bobbins constantly when you change the upper thread color to match or contrast with the appliqué piece.

It also helps to use an embroidery appliqué presser foot on your sewing machine. This foot is scooped out on its underside, allowing it to climb over satin stitches without jamming.

The width of the satin stitch you use will depend on the weight and size of the ap-

pliqué piece you are working with: the smaller the appliqué piece, the narrower the width of the stitch.

Work slowly at first, until you are comfortable satin stitching. When I appliqué, I position my fingers close to each side of the presser foot on the fabric, making an arch with each hand; this gives me maximum control to turn, move, and guide the fabric as I stitch. After years of appliquéing I still stitch slowly around small pieces. Sometimes I stitch over a design a second time to make it look more satiny. Cotton thread fills in much better than polyester thread. You may choose to set the zigzag stitch far apart the first time, then go over it a second time with a closer stitch. This is a very durable way to appliqué.

Use embroidery or specialty appliqué scissors (Figure I-4) to carefully trim "shaggy" areas.

Hand Appliqué

Hand appliqué gives shapes a sculptured, softer look. It is more fragile and less durable than machine stitching, so I recommend it only for items made for special occasions. Select fabrics for appliqué with similar fabric content to main garment. Add 1/8" to 1/4" all around the appliqué pattern. Where one piece is tucked under another, increase the allowance to 1/2". You

can pin appliqués in place or hand baste them if there are several pieces. Fold under seam allowances with your fingers as you go. It isn't necessary to have all edges turned or pressed under before you begin— it can be too frustrating. Small, blind-hemming stitches will hold pieces in place.

You will note none of the projects in this book use this hand appliqué method. As baby items require lots of laundering, I find machine appliqué better able to withstand frequent trips to the washing machine.

Machine Quilting

Baste top, batting, and backing together. If it is a small area, pins can hold the layers in place. Set your machine to straight stitch with approximately 10 stitches per inch. Machine stitch 1/4" from the seam or sew right in the seam (stitch-in-the-ditch). If you are sewing right in the seam, using a zipper foot attachment will help you sew accurately. Continually check the backing or lining—sometimes it will pucker because of the loft of the batting. I place both my hands flat on each side of the presser foot and gently guide the fabric. The best way to prevent the layers from creeping is to use a walking foot attachment, available from your sewing machine dealer. When you have finished a section, pull the top thread to the back and knot securely. Thread ends through a needle, hand stitch 2" to 3" away, then clip threads. Start each section in the middle, and always stitch toward the outside edges, since the lining can move as you stitch.

Hand Quilting

The soft, "loving hands" look of a hand-quilted garment or baby quilt shows that time and care went into each stitch.

Baste the three layers together, the same as for machine quilting. I prefer the durability of quilting thread, and it won't tangle as much as regular thread. A hoop or small frame to hold your project taut is optional. Knot a single thread, 18" long. Quilting needles are very sharp and move through fabrics more easily than standard sewing needles. A thimble is optional.

While true quilt traditionalists stitch 12 – 15 evenly spaced stitches per inch, please don't consider yourself a failure if your stitches aren't comparable. If you are able to manage 6-8 stitches per inch, your results will be lovely. It's more important to quilt with uniform, **even** stitches for a quality look than to quilt with tiny stitches.

Outline quilt the layers of fabric together to highlight the shape of the design. Sew directly on top of the seam line of your project or close to each side of it, using thread to match or blend with the fabric. Catch all layers with each stitch, using a small running stitch. To finish the thread, pull it to the wrong side, knot, and slip the needle horizontally through lining to underside; cut thread close to lining fabric.

Hand quilting stitches can also be placed parallel to a seam, or you may want to quilt a design in a "blank" area.

♥ Machine Basting

If you baste or sew gathering stitches by machine, set the machine for a long, straight stitch and loosen the tension slightly. Then pull the bobbin thread, either to gather the fabric or to remove basting stitches when seam is completed. There are now basting threads available that will dissolve when the item is laundered. It's worthwhile to experiment with this thread as it can save you time.

When gathering pieces (ruffles, full skirts or pants, cap sleeves, etc.), I prefer to zigzag stitch over a cord (such as buttonhole twist thread); then pull cord to gather material, adjusting gathers evenly; and remove cord after the gathers are permanently stitched in place. This method eliminates problems with gathering stitches which sometimes snap and break.

♥ Helpful Hints

For the best results when laundering cotton or acrylic sweaters that have been appliquéd, be sure to turn the sweaters inside out to protect them from snagging on other items in your washer.

I always had mixed feelings as my children grew: it meant that I could have a wonderful time making them new clothes to wear, but it also meant that the clothes that I loved were not going to be worn any more. There are some great solutions, though, to the outgrown clothing problem.

Some of the items you have made are like a photograph album—memories abound. A lovingly made christening dress, bonnet, or bib can be stored in acid-free tissue for generations to come. One of my daughter's bibs that was shadow-appliquéd and trimmed with exquisite embroidery and lace is now framed and sits over my drafting table. When I gaze at that bib, I can't help but smile. Don't feel guilty when you can't part with certain baby items—they are a part of your life and deserve to be carefully saved and cherished.

There is a lot of built-in growing room in children's wear, especially if you make it yourself. Add extra length to the hems of jumpers, pants, and so on, so that you can let down hems as children grow. You can add tucks for growing room which can be removed to give added life to an item. If you are faced with telltale lines from the tucks or hems, stitch rows of middy braid or rickrack over the lines to camouflage them.

Also keep in mind that a jumper is not always a jumper—it can also be a pinafore or sundress. Use it as a top over a pair of simple pants to make a charming outfit. Coordinate the jumper with a pair of matching bloomers underneath. Trim the bloomers with a small appliqué that matches the jumper and you have a special outfit for another season.

My daughter had a pair of appliquéd Oshkosh overalls that she loved to wear and was heartbroken when they were too short. I added an elastic casing to the bottom hems and they became knickers. We added a pair of red and white striped knee socks, and she fell in love with the outfit all over again. Because of the growing room that was built into the straps, her overalls could be worn for another year.

When clothes are just **too** small, lend them to a friend with children who wear smaller sizes. Because of the sturdy quality of garments you have made, they will look great for a long time. Sharing hand-me-downs increases the value of the clothing you made, and they'll be viewed by the recipients as treasures, rather than old clothes.

Some of the baby/toddler clothing left over may be a bit too worn or slightly stained and not acceptable to pass along to family or friends. It is still serviceable. Launder and stack these items in a box and put them on the shelf. Once children have stuffed animals and dolls who are in dire need of wardrobes, that carton of clothing will win hearts all over again.

After you've shared the clothes, and they've been returned, you can recycle them into crazy quilts by cutting around appliquéd sections and arranging them into an eye-appealing design. Piece them together, add a border, and back the quilt with a complementary fabric. Your crazy quilt will also become a memory quilt; you'll have a special time with your children, recalling all the fun they had wearing the clothes.

♥ *Supplies and Tools*

The supplies and tools listed are suggestions to guide you in making the clothing shown in this book. The materials listed are the ones that were used to create the projects as photographed. Always feel free to use what works best for you. Use the supplies, tools, and materials lists as guidelines, not absolute requirements. The most helpful suggestion I can give you is to use what you have on hand and **improvise.** To do so can result in wonderful clothing you will be proud to say you created yourself.

Scissors

Scissors are one of the most important tools a seamstress owns. Keep two pairs on hand: one for paper and one for fabrics. My special pair of sewing scissors has a red ribbon tied in a bow on the handle to alert me to use it only for fabric.

Embroidery or appliqué scissors (Figure I-4) are ideal for cutting out small shapes, snipping curves and corners, and cutting into hard-to-reach areas. The curve of appliqué scissors is especially handy for snipping off excess threads that were not caught in the stitching.

Rotary cutters are excellent for cutting several layers at a time. You can stack three to four light- or medium-weight fabrics and cut them at one time. Always use a cutting mat under fabrics when using a rotary cutter. To save time trim seam allowances to 1/4" while you cut out garments with a rotary cutter or razor edge scissors.

Pins and Needles

One of the best purchases I made was a magnetic pin catcher that adheres to my sewing machine. I can easily pull out pins as I stitch and have them caught in one handy place without sacrificing sewing speed or quality. A freestanding magnetic pin catcher is also ideal and can double as a paperweight. I also use mine to hold handy tools such as a seam ripper, appliqué scissors, and tiny safety pins.

Extra long quilting pins are a great help for multilayered projects. When working with knits, use ballpoint pins that gently maneuver the knit rather than fighting it. An assortment of hand and sewing machine needles is a good investment: you can determine your favorite size, but will probably use them all for one project or another. Crewel needles (especially #10) are handy for embroidered touches.

Ballpoint hand-sewing needles make hand sewing with knits a breeze, rather than a tug-of-war. Look for them in packages offering a wide size range at your sewing store's notions rack.

When doing machine appliqué, be sure your needles are sharp and the correct size for the fabric you are working with, so as not to overstress and pull the fabrics. I most often use a size 12 (80) for machine appliqué, especially for fabrics such as Trigger or sailcloth. When sewing any projects using knits, be sure to use a ballpoint sewing machine needle for best results.

Threads

When sewing clothes for children of any age, sturdy construction is a must. Use poly/cotton thread for main construction and extra fine 100% cotton thread for machine appliqué stitches. If you find good quality white or off-white thread on sale, buy several spools. It is excellent for a standard bobbin thread when doing machine appliqué. After a long process of trial and error, I am especially fond of the quality of Metrosene and Molnlycke threads. But once again, use the brand that works best for you on your machine.

Fabrics

When yardages are given in a materials list, I have assumed that the fabric is at least 44" wide. Preshrink all fabrics as soon as you get home from the store so that you are always ready to begin a project at a moment's notice.

Try to use fabrics of common fiber content: this will prevent one fabric from shrinking or colors from running, which can ruin the appliqué and the outfit. If your main fabric choice is poly/cotton, use appliqué pieces in poly/cotton or cotton.

When sewing for newborns to toilet-trained tots, I prefer to stick with 100% cotton whenever possible. Yes, cotton does shrink—hence the preshrinking information. And yes, 100% cotton can be a little more expensive. But, my preference is based on one important factor: 100% cotton breathes. With babies and toddlers, you can always plan that several times a day, for a variety of reasons, the child will be wet. With 100% cotton fabrics, the baby is less likely to get harmful rashes or have irritation problems with the fabrics. And now there are 100% cottons on the market that are permanent-press.

Select a lofty needle-punched fleece when batting or fleece is called for in the materials list. This weight adds warmth without bulk—especially nice for children's garments. This type of batting will not beard when you quilt—another plus. If you want to add loft to a project, sandwich thicker polyester or cotton batting between two pieces of lightweight fusible interfacing and fuse together. This method will both keep the thicker batting from bearding and keep it from getting caught in your machine's presser foot when sewing on batting alone if you are simply quilting fabric with no backing.

Knit Knacks

Garments for babies and toddlers must be able to withstand squirming and scooting, kicking and cuddling. Knit fabrics and trims are an excellent choice as they can stretch and give to accommodate movement. With the beautiful variety of colors and textures, along with knit ribbings and tapes, a knit wardrobe for youngsters can create a comfortable and upscale look.

You've never sewn with knits before? Don't worry; it's easy. With a basic supply of specialty notions and a few tips, you'll find knits can be used with commercial patterns for both stretch and woven fabrics. A minimal investment in ballpoint sewing machine needles, ballpoint pins (with glass heads—these are easier to use and you can find them in the carpet!), and ballpoint hand-sewing needles are a must. These needles and pins wedge gently into the knit, gliding easily into the fabric.

I apply red nail polish to the top shaft of all my ballpoint sewing machine needles so I can easily find them in my sewing box. My ballpoint hand-sewing needles and ballpoint pins are found only in my red tomato pincushion. This easy system helps organize your knit specialty notions.

As with any variety of fabric, there is a wide range of quality available. Once again, 100% cotton knits are the optimal choice. You can also find excellent quality poly/cotton blends. Use your senses when selecting the knit: **touch** the fabric—rub the knit on the inside of your wrist to see if the fabric is soft and nonabrasive; **smell** the fabric—a fishy odor can result from sizing that won't always wash out; **look** at the fabric piece carefully— inspecting for needle holes, permanent fold lines, and flaws. Also, not all knits are 60" wide; check bolt ends for width and fabric content.

Preshrink all knits as you would any fabric and dry twice in your dryer to preshrink. By drying fabrics twice, you assure fabric has shrunk as much as possible before making garments. Cotton interlocks can shrink up to 25%, so this step is essential. I add a cup of clear vinegar to my wash water to set all colors, as surprises are not fun later.

The ribbing used in all the projects of this book is 100% cotton and was preshrunk. While you do not normally preshrink ribbing, it is important to do so here because the ribbing pieces you are using for a baby are quite small. If you don't preshrink 100% cotton ribbing, you may not be able to fit a baby's hand or foot through openings.

Should your knit piece have a permanent fold line, refold as necessary so fold line will be cut away and discarded. Follow "with nap" layouts given with your pattern whenever possible. Otherwise you might lay out pieces across the grain and have the stretch going the wrong way.

When stitching knits, switch to a ball-point sewing machine needle, adjust your machine for stretch stitch, and set stitch length for 8-10 stitches per inch. If you have problems with knit edges jamming in your machine when you start stitching a seam, place a scrap of tear-away interfacing or double thickness of tissue paper under edge (between sewing machine and fabric), and stitch. After stitching, remove interfacing (or paper) and discard.

If you haven't pretrimmed seam allowances to 1/4" when cutting out your garment, grade seams to 1/4" after sewing seams. Don't clip around curves as this method will leave impressions on right side of garment and may weaken seam.

Stabilize the knit area with lightweight fusible interfacing when you are planning to appliqué on a knit background. Apply interfacing to **wrong** side of knit **underneath** appliqué area. This will prevent the knit from stretching or puckering when you appliqué your design in place.

Bias, Binding Strips, and Piping

The more I use bias or binding strips, the more I love them. This quick way of finishing raw edges can add a dash of color most effectively. When combined with flat piping, corded piping, or rickrack, bias or knit binding can pull a garment together.

Most fabric stores offer an assortment of bias tape colors and widths. Piping comes in rainbow colors, available by the yard or in packages of 2 – 3 yards.

Another consideration is making your own bias tape, knit binding strips, flat piping, and corded piping. I'll admit, at first

I was skeptical about the time and hassle of this prospect. But I love the variety of choices I can have when I make these notions myself from my scrap bag, with very little effort required. If you use the following instructions, I think you'll agree.

Piping (flat or corded) and binding tape can be made from either woven or knit fabrics. Prewash all fabrics chosen for these trims to assure they're colorfast and will not shrink any further. Cut woven fabric on the bias; knit fabrics are cut on crosswise or lengthwise grain. When choosing a fabric for your trims, select one that is similar in fabric content to the project you are sewing. For filled piping, you may use either cording or yarn; preshrink materials before using in piping.

Binding Strip Technique

1. Cut strips 1½" wide.

2.

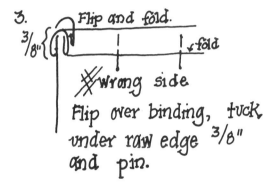

   right side

   With right sides together, stitch with ³/₈" seam allowance.

3. Flip and fold.

   ³/₈" { fold

   wrong side

   Flip over binding, tuck under raw edge ³/₈" and pin.

4. Machine stitch ¹/₁₆" from folded edge.

Fig. I-5

or Hand stitch with blind hem stitch.

My width preference for bias/binding strips for most purposes is 1-1/2". This width makes a double-fold binding 3/8" wide. Cut one end of binding strip at an angle and pull through bias strip maker. Press folds in place as the strip comes out folded from the tape maker. To piece strips, pin strips in V-shape at 90 degree angle. With right sides together and short ends aligned, stitch seam and trim ends evenly with the binding strip. The binding technique used throughout the layette is illustrated in Figure I-5.

Piping can be flat or filled. For flat piping, cut strips 1" wide (woven fabric on bias; knit fabrics on crosswise or lengthwise grain). Fold with wrong sides together lengthwise and lightly press. Filled piping works well with 1-1/2" strips. Fold lengthwise with wrong sides together and center cording or yarn along inside fold, enclosing filler. Using a zipper foot attachment, stitch close to cording with matching thread. For best results, stretch fabric slightly as you sew.

An additional notion that I refer to frequently is invisible elastic. This is a new type of elastic that is clear and colorless, appearing to disappear when sewn to fabric. Invisible elastic is lightweight, can stretch to more than double its original length, and can be sewn to fabric without affecting the original stretch. One time-saving technique is to stretch elastic along wrist and stitch directly onto the stretched invisible elastic, eliminating the need for casings.

Notion Know-How for Appliqué

After years of appliquéing everything from bonnets to booties, I have found backing all appliqué fabrics with lightweight fusible interfacing to work best. It is easiest to fuse the interfacing to the wrong side of fabric pieces first, and then cut out the appliqué. Most fabric shops have lightweight interfacing available in packages of 3 yards for a very reasonable price; I used Pellon's interfacing for this book. Three 3-yard packages will make all of the projects in this book. The interfacing stabilizes the fabrics so they do not pucker or fray, yet does not make the appliqué too bulky. This is especially important for appliquéing more than one layer.

Another trick to retard fraying of appliqué pieces is to use spray starch on appliqué pieces before cutting out. This step gives the fabric a crisp, sized finish that also makes the appliqué piece more substantial and easier to appliqué.

The fastest method for fused appliqués is using paper-backed fusible webbing such as Aleene's Hot Stitch Fusible Web or Pellon's Wonder-Under. Please keep in mind that these are not interfacings, but rather bonding materials. Test a small area first to be sure your fabric is compatible with this method. Follow the step-by-step instructions that come with the fusible webbing for best results.

♥ *Tip:* Shapes drawn on paper backing of fusible web will be reversed on the garment. Therefore, draw mirror images of letters or numbers.

Glues

With good nonsoluble glues on the market, a lot of busy work can be cut down. Thoroughly read all the information on the glue containers to be sure it will work for the project you are making. Hot glue guns and glue sticks are excellent for nursery decor items. However, I do not advise gluing trims to baby or toddlerwear for children under three years of age. Tiny fingers are strong and can pull off trims—turning them into munchables.

To help make appliqué even easier, there are now glue sticks and fabric glues that will hold pieces in place and then wash out after laundering. One interesting discovery I made is that fabric glue sticks are essentially the same as the kind sold in stationery stores—at a considerably lower price. A good rule of thumb is to test the glues on scraps before using them for your garment. Using scraps from your garment, glue same scrap fabric to sample. Wash and dry this sample to see if any glue residue remains on the fabrics, if the fabrics are discolored in any way, or if the fabrics become stiff after laundering. By testing a sample, you eliminate the risk of ruining a garment on which you have spent considerable time and money.

Pens, Pencils, and Paints

Have on hand a few soft number 2 pencils and a package of good quality white tissue paper, which is available in stationery or discount stores. These are needed for tracing patterns. Air-soluble or water-soluble marking pens make detail embroidery work and topstitching a snap. Using the baby bunny appliqué pattern (Figure 1-7) as an example, you can draw in the leg topstitching detail and facial features shown, and dampen the area to dissolve either pen should you be displeased with first efforts.

If you are pleased with markings, proceed to topstitch, embroider, or paint details, and have the markings dissolve. I prefer the disappearing ink (air-soluble) marking pen whose ink evaporates within 48 hours. However, if you find you are able to sew only in hourly time slots, you'll find the water-soluble pen the better choice.

If you dislike embroidery work, consider hand painting detail using acrylic paints. For children's clothing that is frequently laundered, allow paints to dry 24 hours and permanently set paints by using a pressing cloth and steam iron set on "cotton" to iron over painted area.

The new bottles of Tulip Paints on the market cover everything from fluorescent colors, to glitter paints, to puffy paints, to bright crayon box Slick paints. They are easy to use, offer an incredible palette of colors, and launder beautifully. However, do not heat set these paints with the above method as the paints will melt. Follow the instructions given on the package.

I do not recommend using puffy paints for children under the age of three as their little hands can pull off the raised paints and toddlers may promptly eat the paint. While the paints are nontoxic, it's better to be safe than sorry.

♥ *Additional Embellishments*

Detail can be added to baby and toddler garments in several ways. If you are not comfortable painting details, embroidery may work better for you. Draw in details needed with fabric pens and embroider in appropriate colors. Brief diagrams are included for simple embroidery stitches (Figure I-6).

Ribbons come in every color, design, and width imaginable. For the multi-looped bows used throughout the book, follow the directions in Figure I-7.

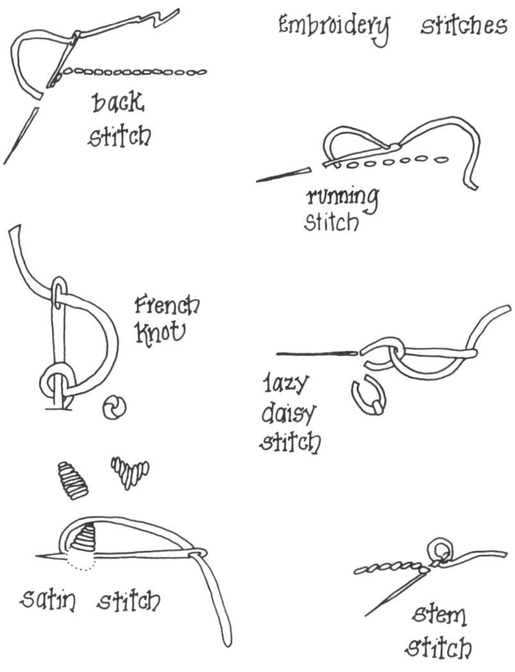

Embroidery stitches

back stitch

running stitch

French knot

lazy daisy stitch

satin stitch

stem stitch

Fig. I-6

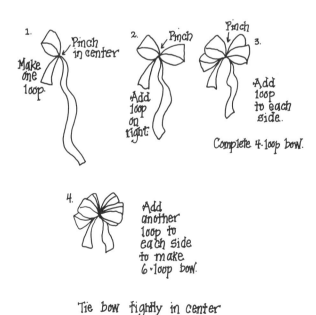

To make 4-loop and 6-loop bows:

1. Make one loop. Pinch in center

2. Add loop on right. Pinch

3. Pinch. Add loop to each side. Complete 4-loop bow.

4. Add another loop to each side to make 6-loop bow.

Tie bow tightly in center or sew through center to hold.

Fig. I-7

♥ Shopping Hints

The very best advice I can offer is to watch for sales! Look for discounts on notions and stock up on threads, bias tape, ribbon, and buttons. Write approximate yardages needed for basics like pants, shirts, jumpers, and jackets on an index card and tuck it in your wallet. When you come across a good reduction on mini-dot prints, poplin solids, gingham, Trigger, quality knits, or other favorite staples, you'll be prepared to stock up on a rainbow assortment of colors in correct amounts. Because infant and toddler wear requires such minimal yardage, check the remnant tables for bargains, too. Scraps of fabric you might already have from other projects are ideal for trims, facings, or appliqués. (Be sure they, too, are preshrunk.)

Savings in end-of-season sales on sweaters, solid-color sweatsuits, and accessories can be substantial. When you have a favorite brand of sweater or jacket, guess approximate size needs for the upcoming year and stock up when you see the items reduced at season's end.

For adding those all-important wardrobe accessories, chain discount stores are a wonderful source for staples to which you can add special embellishments. Packages containing three pairs of cotton-knit anklets or cable-knit knee socks can be purchased for a fraction of the price of one pair at a fancy boutique. Dime stores offer a treasure trove of delights, such as ribbon bundle specials and assortments of buttons or snaps at a discount.

Women's specialty stores and avant-garde stationery shops sometimes carry an extraordinary line of imported ribbons and buttons. When I find a special ribbon that I can't live without, my rule of thumb is to buy three yards: enough for pigtails or shoelaces and to spur my imagination at a later date.

♥ *Rx for Care:* Avoid the excessive use of buttons, bells, pompoms, and other "munchables" for children under the age of three. Toddlers usually inspect their clothing with small, curious hands, so secure any trims with extra care. I can offer two tips to help here: use dental floss to secure buttons on fabrics that are sturdy. The floss is so strong that lightweight fabrics will rip before the buttons come off—use only on strong, tightly woven fabrics. Another way to help secure buttons for little ones is to stitch them on using elastic thread. It will stretch when pulled and cannot easily be pulled off the garment.

Part 1

♥ *To the Manor Born* ♥

1. *Layette*

I'll be the first to admit that our lives in the 1990s can be described in a single word: B-U-S-Y. Yet the idea of sewing for an expected or new baby is often the exception to the statement "I don't have enough time to sew." Why? Because sewing for infants touches a basic nurturing instinct and because it's just plain fun! Layette items such as bibs, blankets, hooded towels, and buntings require only the simplest of sewing skills.

In this chapter are directions for a love basket to be used as a special shower gift along with a music box cottage; basic layette items for both boys and girls, using a bunny appliqué or a fabric rosebud as a coordinating detail; a variety of bath-time items, also personalized by the bunny or rosebud; and some clothing enlivened by a simple bear shape.

Fig. 1-1

♥ Layette
Love Basket
Music Box Cottage

♥ Bunny
Jumpsuit
Reversible Cap
Monogrammed Anklets
Reversible Bib
Rattles

♥ Rosebud
Nightgown
Reversible Bib
Rattles
Headband
Anklets
Receiving Blanket

Burp Pad
Bunting
Booties
Straw Hat

♥ Bath-time Boutique
Appliquéd Washcloths
Diaper Changing Pad
Wash Mitts
Hooded Towel

♥ Bear Boutique
Girl's Romper
Boy's Romper
Cardigan Sweater
Rattle
Appliquéd and Pieced Bib

♥ *Oh Baby!*

Layette Bundle of Love Basket

Fig. 1-2

You've been invited to a baby shower for someone quite special, and you would like your gift presentation to express your feelings of joy for the new parents. Here is the perfect answer—a bundle of love basket. Fill this quick yet classy basket with some of the layette projects shown here or stop at the local market and buy an assortment of lotions, diapers, and bottles. Don't forget to include a treat or two for the new mom: a bestselling paperback, travel-size toiletries for her maternity stay, or the latest issue of her favorite magazine.

♥ *Note:* If you have trouble with glue not holding doilies in place during gluing process, use spring-type clothespins to hold doilies in place until secure.

Materials

10" diameter x 4" deep whitewashed basket (with handle, 12" high)

6 8" white Battenberg lace doilies (available at linen outlets, discount stores, or through J.C. Penney)

6" white Battenberg lace doily

3 yards 1/16" white satin ribbon

1 yard 5/8" white sheer stripe picot ribbon

1 yard 6" white tulle

Can of spray starch

Aleene's Tacky glue

Matching threads

Optional: Clothespins

Directions

1. Spray starch all Battenberg lace doilies. Cut 8" doilies in half, fold down cut edge 1/4", and press. Sew narrow 1/8" hem along cut edge of half doilies, overlapping doily edges to string all doilies together.

2. Set sewing machine for widest possible zigzag stitch. Place 1/16" white satin ribbon 3/4" from folded, hemmed edge of the doily string and zigzag over the ribbon. Take care **not** to catch ribbon in the zigzag stitching.

3. Pull ribbon to gather at ends. Between sixth and seventh doily, pull ribbon to gather. When doilies are gathered enough to fit top edge of basket, adjust gathers evenly. Fit doily ruffle to outside basket edge, and tie ribbons into bows at handles. Trim off excess ribbon and set aside. Glue gathered seam to top edge of basket.

4. Wrap tulle loosely around basket handle. Use remaining 1/16" white satin ribbon left from gathering doilies to tie tulle to handles at 2-3" intervals. Tie ribbon in bows and trim ribbon ends as necessary. Fluff out tulle for frothy look, using photo as a guide.

5. For elaborate bow on handle, spray starch 6" Battenberg lace doily. Fold doily in half and crease. Stitch row of gathering stitches along crease and gather; knot securely. Make a six-loop bow of 5/8" white sheer stripe picot ribbon and tack to gathered center of doily. Cut 8" piece of 1/16" white satin ribbon and set aside. With remaining white satin ribbon, fold into multiloop bow and tie to center of sheer

stripe and Battenberg doily bow. Securely tie bow to handle with 8" length of ribbon previously cut. Fill basket with goodies.

Music Box Cottage

Fig. 1-3

Rock-a-bye baby will sleep with sweet dreams with this charming music box cottage to lull your tot to sleep. You'll be pleasantly surprised at how easy it is to stitch this accessory with loving hands and heart.

Materials

"Wind up" music box hardware— choose a soothing tune such as "Lara's Theme", "Send in the Clowns," or "You Light up My Life."

1/4 yard light blue/white double-sided with reverse print quilted floral fabric

Scraps of:

  2 pastel mini-prints to coordinate with quilted fabric

  Aleene's Hot Stitch Fusible Web

  1/2" white ruffled eyelet lace

  1/2" white picot ribbon

  1/2" white flat lace trim

  Medium-sized pink rickrack

  Polyfil batting and stuffing

3 white satin rosebud flowers

Pink 1/4" heart button

1/3 yard 5/8" white sheer stripe picot ribbon

Matching threads

Directions

1. Back pastel mini-print scraps with Aleene's Hot Stitch Fusible Web. Cut out pieces for cottage as follows (see Figure 1-4):

  two main houses, one roof, one door, quilted fabric
  two shutters, one door window, pastel mini-print
  one gable, two house windows, other pastel mini-print

2. Attach white reverse print for roof to blue front house piece, while zigzag stitching white flat lace along bottom edge of roof. Position, fuse, and use a medium-width zigzag to satin stitch the door to the front house piece.

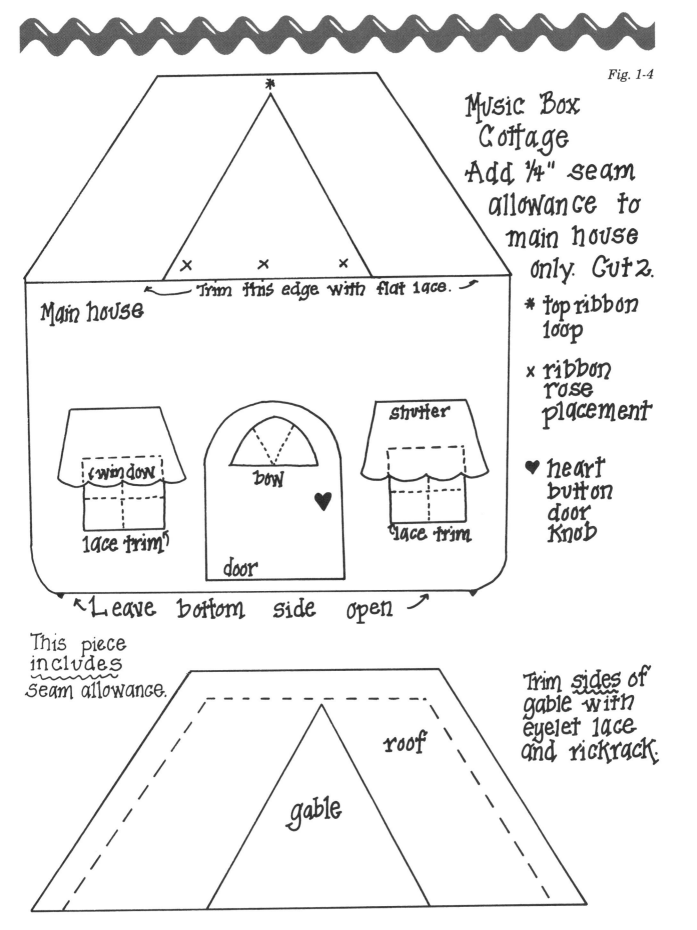

Fig. 1-4

Music Box
Cottage
Add ¼" seam
allowance to
main house
only. Cut 2.

Main house

Trim this edge with flat lace.

* top ribbon loop

× ribbon rose placement

♥ heart button door knob

window

lace trim

bow

♥

shutter

lace trim

door

Leave bottom side open

This piece includes seam allowance.

Trim sides of gable with eyelet lace and rickrack.

roof

gable

3. Peel off paper backing from small appliqués, position and fuse roof gable, door window, shutters, and windows following Figure 1-4. Use a narrow-width zigzag to satin stitch the appliqué pieces with matching threads. Stitch flat lace trim to bottom of house windows. Tie bow of white picot ribbon and tack under door window. Sew pink heart button in place for doorknob.

4. Trim top peak of roof gable with eyelet lace and pink rickrack as shown in the photo. Tack three white satin rosebuds evenly across lower bottom edge of gable. Fold 12" piece of white sheer stripe picot ribbon in half and baste ends to top of roof.

5. Assemble music box with wind-up key and test to be sure it works well. Position so music box is in middle of house and mark house back piece with key position. Stitch 3/4" buttonhole at key position and slit carefully. Unscrew key from hardware.

6. Pin lace ruffle at gable top toward bottom of house front so it won't be caught in stitching. With right sides together, pin and stitch around house, using 1/4" seam allowance, leaving open at bottom. Clip corners and turn right side out.

7. Wrap polyfil batting around music box to cushion it, taking care not to cover spot for key. Stuff top of cottage with polyfil, insert music box in house and position so you can screw in key. Adjust position as necessary and stuff firmly with polyfil batting. Sew bottom closed with tiny overcast stitches. Unpin lace at gable top and fluff. Screw in music box key.

♥ *Note:* Due to decorative trims used on this project, please **don't** hand this music box to baby or place in crib where baby can reach. Instead, place box on dresser top, in baby's accessory basket, or hang from wall or door knob.

♥ *Baby Boy's Bunny Boutique*

(See Color Pages)

Fig. 1-5

This ensemble of clothing and accessories is all simple to stitch, and easy on the budget, too. Using a motif featuring appliquéd bunnies in a light blue/white color scheme, you can mix and match mini-dot prints, stripes, and solids to create an upscale look. Because the bunny appliqué is used to coordinate jumpsuit, reversible cap, and reversible bib plus bath-time items, separate instructions are given here for this appliqué design.

(above) Rose appliqués on towel, washcloths, and bath mitt (Chapter 1)

(right) Bunny appliqués on Hooded Towel and Jazzy Jumpsuit; Bunny Wrist Rattle (Chapter 1)

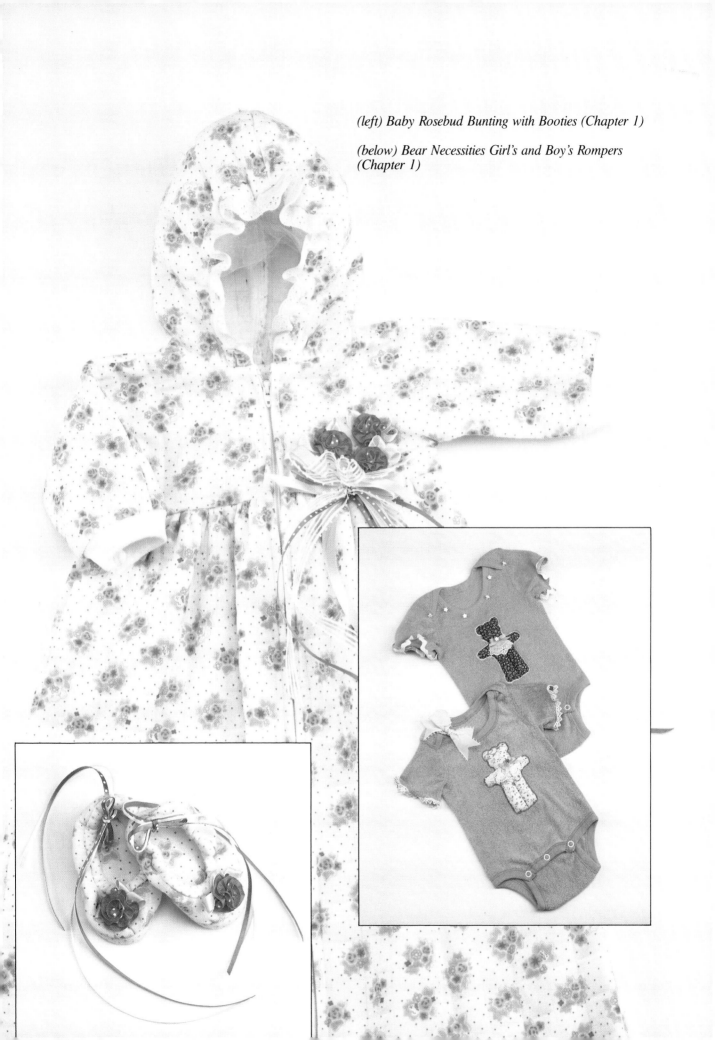

(left) Baby Rosebud Bunting with Booties (Chapter 1)

*(below) Bear Necessities Girl's and Boy's Rompers
(Chapter 1)*

(clockwise, top left) Back-to-School Apple Tabard, Clowning Around Terry Bib, This Lil' Piggy Cover-up Bib, Loch Mess Monster Cover-up Bib (Chapter 2)

Bunny Appliqué

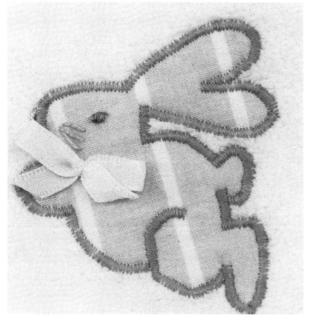

Fig. 1-6

Materials

Note: Each 1/8 yard will make 10 bunny appliqués.

1/8 yard light blue with white stripe chintz (called "blue appliqué")

1/8 yard white with light blue stripe chintz (called "white appliqué")

1 yard each: 1/4" white and light blue satin ribbon

1/4 yard lightweight iron-on interfacing

Package Aleene's Hot Stitch Fusible Web

Embroidery floss in light blue and pink

Disappearing ink marking pen

Matching threads

Directions

1. Prewash chintz fabrics and press. Back chintz pieces with lightweight iron-on interfacing. Trace bunnies (Figure 1-7) on paper backing of Aleene's Hot Stitch Fusible Web and fuse to wrong side of chintz stripe. Cut out eight light blue and four white bunny appliqués. It doesn't matter where the stripe falls; do what looks good to you.

2. With the disappearing ink marking pen, draw eye, whiskers and topstitching detail for the leg. (If you're not pleased with your first efforts, erase ink by dampening lines. Allow to dry thoroughly and try again.) Peel off paper backing and position as directed in each project. Fuse in place.

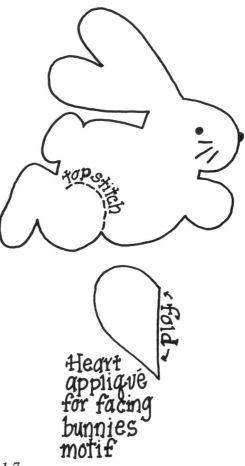

Bunny Appliqué
(can be reversed)

top stitch

Heart appliqué for facing bunnies motif

fold

Fig. 1-7

3. Appliqué with medium-width satin stitch and continue to satin stitch the leg detail. Embroider eye with two strands of light blue embroidery floss in satin stitch. Using two strands of pink floss, embroider nose with satin stitch and whiskers with long straight stitch. Lightly press.

4. Fold double-loop bow and gather through center of bow; knot securely. Tack bow at bunny's neck. Peel up and trim excess interfacing around wrong side of appliqué.

♥ *Sewing Hint:* When sewing bunny appliqué to knit fabrics, be sure to switch to a ballpoint sewing machine needle. Back piece to be appliquéd with lightweight iron-on interfacing **underneath** appliqué area to stabilize knit. When stitching bunny appliqué to terry cloth, use tear-away interfacing or several layers of tissue paper underneath appliqué on wrong side of project. This stabilizes the terry and will keep it from stretching; also, this method will help keep threads and loops from underside of terry from being caught in the feed dogs.

Jazzy Jumpsuit

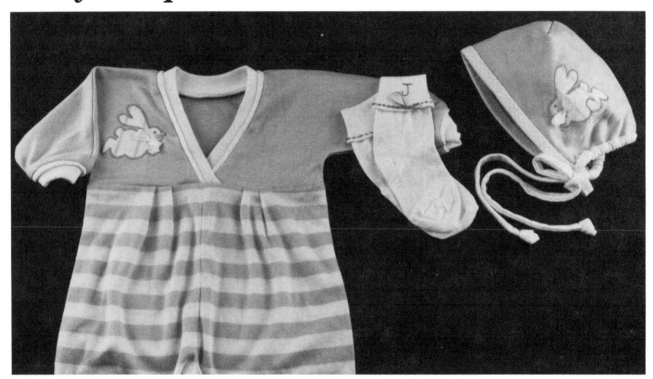

Fig. 1-8

♥ *Note:* Adjust amounts of cotton knit fabrics, ribbing, and snap tape as needed according to pattern requirements and size. Yardages given here will make up to 12-month size.

Materials

Jumpsuit pattern (pattern here was Sew Little Layette— see Resource List)

1/4 yard solid light blue cotton knit, 60" wide

1/2 yard light blue/white stripe cotton knit, 60" wide

1/8 yard white with light blue pin dot cotton knit

6" white cotton ribbing

1/2 yard white snap tape

White bunny appliqué facing right (see instructions earlier)

Matching threads

Directions

1. Preshrink all cotton knit fabrics, ribbing, and snap tape. Lightly press as needed. Cut top bodice/sleeves for front and back pieces from light blue solid knit. Cut pant leg pieces in light blue/white stripe knit, taking care to match stripes at side and crotch seams. Following the pattern, cut necessary size ribbing for neckline, sleeve cuffs, and pant cuffs. Cut one strip 1" x 60" of the pin dot knit for flat piping trim. *Note:* To save time, pretrim pieces to 1/4" seam allowance when you cut out your garment if using commercial pattern.

2. Position and sew white bunny appliqué to left side bodice front following the appliqué directions earlier in this chapter. *Note:* If your jumpsuit style has a plain bodice front instead of a V-neck, consider embellishing with facing bunnies with heart or star in center.

3. Using purchased pattern instructions as a guide, stitch shoulder seams, center front, and center back pant seams.

4. To make flat piping, fold 1" x 60" pin dot strip with wrong sides together lengthwise. Baste flat piping cut edges to sleeve ends and neckline, using 1/8" seam allowance. Stretch and stitch ribbing to neckline and sleeve cuffs with 1/4" seam allowance. This method will allow a 1/4" flat piping of pin dot to show at cuff and neckline.

5. Overlap V-neck front as shown on the pattern and baste. Pleat or gather pants front to bodice front and pants back to bodice back. Stitch in place following pattern instructions. Sew underarm/side seams, matching stripes. Trim pant legs with flat piping and ribbing as in Step 4.

6. Stitch snap tape to inner leg seams. Snap legs together and press garment.

Reversible Cap

(See Figure 1-8)

Materials

1/4 yard light blue solid cotton knit, or scraps from jumpsuit

1/4 yard light blue/white stripe cotton knit, or scraps from jumpsuit

1/8 yard white with light blue pin dot cotton knit, or scraps from jumpsuit

White bunny appliqué (see instructions earlier)

Scrap of lightweight iron-on interfacing

1/4 yard 1/4" white (or invisible) elastic

Matching threads

Directions

1. Prewash all cotton knit fabrics. Lightly press as needed. (Trace cap from Figure 2-15.) Cut one each cap from light blue solid and light blue/white stripe cotton fabrics. Cut one strip 1-1/2" x 60" pin dot cotton knit for binding strips.

2. Position and fuse left-facing bunny appliqué to light blue solid cap on right side. Cut piece of lightweight iron-on interfacing larger than appliqué and fuse to wrong side of blue cap piece underneath appliqué to stabilize knit. Appliqué bunny to cap.

3. Using 1/4" seam allowance, sew center back cap seam. Fold cap for crown seam with center back seam in middle and stitch. Repeat for other cap piece. Pin and baste caps with wrong sides together, using 1/8" seam allowance at neckline and facial opening. Using binding strip, stitch strip to trim facial opening with 3/8" seam allowance. Fold trim around and under 3/8" and stitch binding closed with hand or machine stitches. Cut 36" length of binding strip. Pin-mark at 18" center point to center back seam at neckline. Sew binding to neckline, encasing neckline edge. Thread 9" elastic piece through binding for casing, tacking ends of elastic at cap front sides. Blind stitch or machine stitch ties to make 3/8"-wide ties. Knot ends. Lightly press.

Monogrammed Cotton Anklets

(See Figure 1-8)

Materials

Pair purchased white cotton anklets

1 yard 1/16" light blue satin ribbon

Light blue embroidery floss

Disappearing ink marking pen

Scrap of tear-away interfacing

Blunt needlepoint needle

Directions

1. Prewash socks. Fold cuffs in place. With disappearing ink marking pen, draw first or last initial of baby on outside side of anklet cuff, using basic capital letter print alphabet.

2. With cuff still folded in place, pin small piece of tear-away interfacing to **underside** of anklet ribbing underneath initial. Using two strands of light blue embroidery floss, embroider initial with back stitch, stitching through only one layer of ribbing. Remove interfacing from underside of cuff.

3. Cut two 18" pieces of 1/16" light blue satin ribbon. Thread blunt needlepoint needle with ribbon and start stitching under initial with long straight stitch, 1/4" from edge of anklet cuff. Slightly stretch cuff as you stitch. Take care to keep ribbon flat, not twisted. Continue around sock until you meet the beginning, ending with ribbon stitch on top. Tie ribbon ends in bow.

4. Repeat for other sock.

Reversible Bunny Bib

(See Figure 1-5)

Materials

1/3 yard white cotton terry cloth

1/3 yard light blue/white stripe cotton knit, or scraps from jumpsuit

1/8 yard white with light blue pin dot cotton knit, or scraps from jumpsuit

Blue bunny appliqué, facing left (see instructions earlier)

Scrap of tear-away interfacing

Matching threads

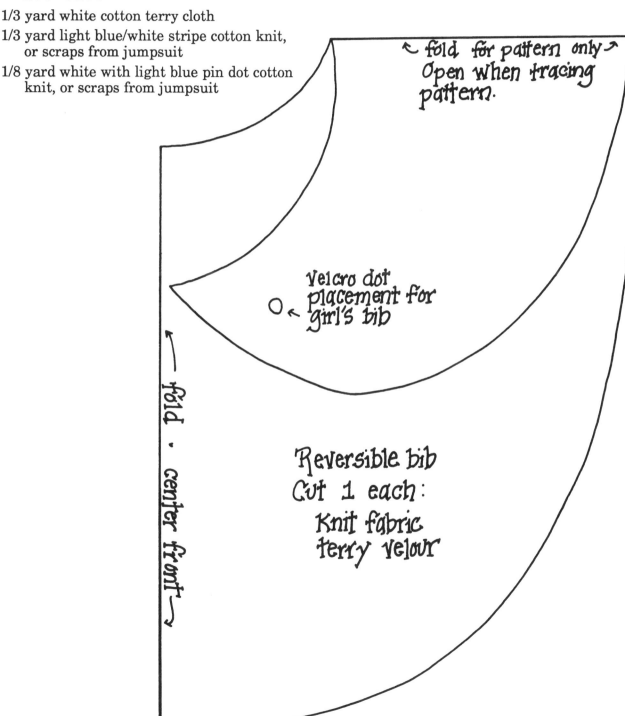

← fold for pattern only →
Open when tracing pattern.

Velcro dot placement for girl's bib

O ←

Reversible bib
Cut 1 each:
Knit fabric
terry velour

← fold · center front →

Fig. 1-9

Directions

1. Prewash terry and cotton knit fabrics; press lightly as necessary. Trace reversible bib pattern (Figure 1-9) onto tissue paper. In order to fit the pattern in the book, I folded it over. Cut one each white terry and light blue/white stripe knit bibs. Cut one strip 1-1/2" x 60" pin dot knit for binding strip.

2. Position and fuse bunny appliqué to center of white terry bib piece. Cut piece of tear-away interfacing slightly larger than appliqué and pin to wrong side of bib **underneath** appliqué. Appliqué bunny to bib with medium-width satin stitch. Trim, following bunny appliqué instructions.

3. Pin and baste terry and knit bibs together with **wrong** sides together. Finish outer edge of bib with binding strip using 3/8" seam allowance. Cut 36" length of knit binding strip and pin-mark at 18" point. Match pin-mark with center front of inner bib neckline. Trim inner bib with knit trim, using 3/8" seam allowance to encase raw edges of inner neckline. Stitch binding ties using either hand blind stitch or machine stitch. Knot bib tie ends. Lightly press.

♥ Bunny Rattles

Fig. 1-10

One of the extra benefits of sewing for youngsters is the ability to take ordinary items and transform them into little tot treasures. A fun example starts with inexpensive purchased rattles available at discount chains or grocery stores. By adding scraps of fabric and trims, you'll love making this set of bunny rattles.

Bunny Wrist Rattle

(See Figure 1-10 and Color Pages)

Materials

1/8 yard white sweatshirt cotton knit fleece

1/8 yard light blue polka dot chintz

Scraps of:

    polyfil stuffing and polyfil batting

    light blue and pink embroidery floss

    1/2" light blue taffeta picot ribbon

2/3 yard 1" light blue dot grosgrain ribbon

6" piece of 3/4" white elastic

Pink Venus colored pencil

Flat oval baby rattle with handle (approx. 2-1/2" oval)

Disappearing ink marking pen

Matching thread

Optional: Use dental floss for secure hold on bow tie and for attaching ribbon bracelet to bunny.

Directions

1. Trace bunny pattern (Figure 1-11) for wrist rattle from book and cut out of tissue paper. Fold sweatshirt piece with fuzzy fleece sides together. Using disappearing ink marking pen, draw around bunny pattern on wrong side of folded fleece knit piece. This is your stitching line.

2. Pin pieces to keep them from shifting and stitch around bunny face along drawn seam line, leaving open between X's. Cut out bunny face with 1/8" seam allowance, turn right side out, and lightly stuff ears. Stitch line of running stitches across ears as shown on the pattern, lightly pull to gather, and knot securely.

3. With disappearing ink marking pen, draw in bunny face as shown on the pattern. With two strands of light blue embroidery floss, embroider eyes with intersecting straight stitches. For heart-shaped nose, satin stitch with two strands of pink embroidery floss.

4. Pull handle off purchased rattle and discard. Stuff top of bunny face. Wrap polyfil batting around flat oval rattle piece and insert in bunny face. Using small tufts of polyfil stuffing, pad area around rattle to cushion. Complete stuffing face and blind stitch bunny closed.

5. Cut two rectangles 4-1/2" x 5-1/2" from light blue polka dot fabric for bow tie. With right sides together, stitch around rectangles with 1/8" seam allowance, leaving 3" opening for turning along one long side. Clip corners, turn right side out, and stitch closed by hand. Find the midpoint of the bow by folding in half, short ends together, and crease. Hand gather along crease to make bow, using dental floss, and double knot. Sew bow tie to bunny's chin very securely—dental floss can be used for this stitching. Tie small bow with light blue picot ribbon and sew to bottom of one ear.

6. Lightly color in cheeks and inner ears with pink Venus colored pencil.

7. Cut 1" wide light blue dot grosgrain ribbon into two 12" pieces. Pin pieces together and stitch ribbons together along 12" edges with a narrow zigzag. Insert elastic into ribbon casing, gather, and zigzag stitch both raw narrow edges together. Tack "ribbon bracelet" to back of bunny face, with zigzag seam facing back of rattle.

Fig. 1-11

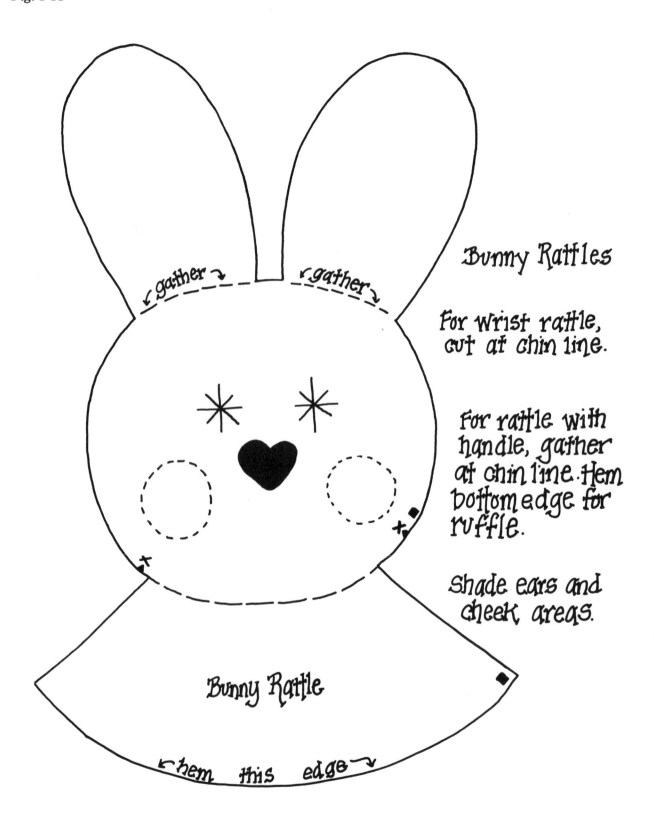

Bunny Rattles

For wrist rattle, cut at chin line.

For rattle with handle, gather at chin line. Hem bottom edge for ruffle.

Shade ears and cheek areas.

gather

gather

Bunny Rattle

hem this edge

Bunny Rattle
with Handle

(See Figure 1-10)

Materials

1/8 yard white sweatshirt cotton knit fleece

1/2 yard 3/8" flat cluny lace

1/2 yard 1/2" white with light blue ribbon

Scraps of:

  polyfil stuffing and polyfil batting

  light blue and pink embroidery floss

Flat oval baby rattle with handle (approx. 2-1/2" oval)

Disappearing ink marking pen

Pink Venus colored pencil

Matching threads (or dental floss for secure hold)

Directions

1. Trace bunny pattern for rattle with handle from book (Figure 1-11) and cut out of tissue paper. Fold sweatshirt piece with fuzzy fleece sides together. Using disappearing ink marking pen, trace around bunny pattern on wrong side of fleece knit piece. This is your stitching line.

2. Pin pieces to keep them from shifting and stitch around bunny face along drawn seam line, leaving open between squares. Cut out bunny face with 1/8" seam allowance, turn right side out, and lightly stuff ears. Stitch line of running stitches across ears as shown on the pattern, lightly pull to gather, and knot securely.

3. With disappearing ink marking pen, draw in bunny face as shown on the pattern. With two strands of light blue embroidery floss, embroider eyes with intersecting straight stitches. For heart-shaped nose, satin stitch with two strands of pink embroidery floss.

4. Stuff top of bunny face. Wrap polyfil batting around flat oval rattle piece and insert in bunny face with handle extending below face. Using small tufts of polyfil stuffing, pad area around rattle to cushion. Hand sew side seam closed and complete stuffing bunny face from the bottom opening. Sew row of hand running stitches at chin line around bunny face, gather tightly, and knot securely. Turn under bottom hem 1/4" and hand stitch while sewing on flat cluny lace.

5. Lightly color in cheeks and inner ears with pink Venus colored pencil.

6. Tie small bow of 1/2" white/light blue ribbon and tack securely to bottom of one ear (use dental floss). With remaining white/light blue ribbon, tie around gathered chin line with bow in front.

♥ *Baby Rosebud Boutique for Girls*

When you are blessed with a girl to sew for, it's hard to resist ribbons, ruffles, and roses. This layette ensemble features projects embellished with a simple flat rose appliqué that even a beginner can stitch with ease. A 3-dimensional ruffled rose is also shown. Once you've mastered this floral frill, you'll enjoy finding places to trim with it. Because the rose appliqué and 3-D rose are used to coordinate all of these projects, separate instructions are given for these trims.

Fig. 1-12

Rose Appliqué

Fig. 1-13

The flat rose appliqué is used to trim items for bath time, as well as the receiving blanket and burp pad. Refer to these instructions when "appliquéd rose" is listed in the materials listing.

Materials

1/8 yard white with pink stripe chintz (called "white chintz"—will make 12 roses)

1/8 yard green pin dot cotton fabric

1/8 yard lightweight iron-on interfacing

Package Aleene's Hot Stitch Fusible Web

Disappearing ink marking pen

Matching threads

Directions

1. Back white chintz and green pin dot with lightweight iron-on interfacing. Draw rose (Figure 1-14) on paper backing of Aleene's Hot Stitch Fusible Web and fuse to wrong side of white chintz, centering the rose over the two stripes. Draw leaf appliqué on paper backing of Aleene's Hot Stitch Fusible Web and fuse in same manner to green dot.

2. Cut out appliqués, peel off paper backing, position, and fuse to project, with rose overlapping leaf as shown on the pattern. With disappearing ink marking pen, draw in swirl design of flower.

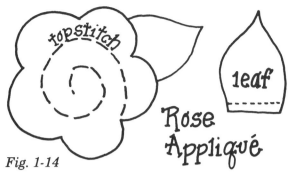

Fig. 1-14

3. Back appliqués with specific interfacing and method as described in each project. Satin stitch with a medium width around the flower. Continue zigzagging for swirl design using contrasting pink thread.

4. Use a medium-width satin stitch and matching thread to appliqué the leaf. Lightly press.

♥ **Sewing Hint:** When sewing rose appliqué to knit fabrics, be sure to switch to a ballpoint sewing machine needle. Back piece to be appliquéd with lightweight iron-on interfacing **underneath** appliqué area to stabilize knit. When stitching rose appliqué to terry cloth, use tear-away interfacing or several layers of tissue paper **underneath** appliqué on wrong side of project. This stabilizes the terry and will keep it from stretching; also, this method will help keep threads and loops on underside of terry from being caught in the feed dogs.

Gathered 3-D Roses

Fig. 1-15

You've seen these lovely flowers trimming everything from designer hats to shoes, children's wear to adult couture. By using cuddly cotton knits or pink dot grosgrain ribbon, you can add this floral frill to tiny finery with beautiful results.

Materials

1/8 yard white with pink pin dot cotton knit

1/8 yard green pin dot cotton fabric

Matching threads

Directions

1. Prewash cotton knit and woven fabrics. Cut white pin dot cotton knit into 1-1/2" x 60" strips. Cut each strip into five 12" lengths. One-eighth yard of cotton knit will make 15 roses.

2. With right sides together, fold strip lengthwise and stitch ends to round off corners as shown on the "rose strip guide" in Figure 1-16. Trim seam allowance to 1/8" and turn right side out.

3. With raw edges and wrong sides together, hand or machine stitch row of gathering stitches along cut length. Pull threads to gather to 5" length and knot. Adjust gathers evenly.

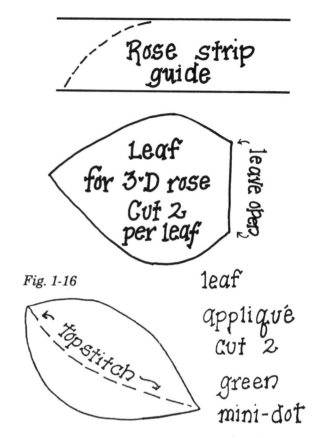

4. Starting at one end, wrap gathered strip around end and tack. This will be the center of the rose. Continue wrapping gathered edges around gathered base, making a tacking stitch every 1/4", tacking each added row to previous one, to end of strip. *Note:* For this size rose, gathered strip will wrap around center approximately three times.

5. Cut two green pin dot leaves (one in reverse) as shown in Figure 1-16. Pin leaf with right sides together and stitch, using 1/8" seam allowance, leaving open as shown on the pattern. Clip corner and turn right side out. Tuck raw edges inside leaf with 1/8" seam allowance and gather. Tack gathered edge of leaf to bottom of cotton knit rose.

Rose strip guide

Leaf for 3-D rose Cut 2 per leaf ← leave open ↙

Fig. 1-16

leaf appliqué cut 2 green mini-dot

← topstitch →

♥ *Note:* Some of the projects are shown with two leaves per cotton knit rose. Simply make two leaves as in Step 5 and stitch them opposite each other to back of cotton knit rose.

Pink Dot Grosgrain Ribbon Roses

Materials

(for one rose)

1/3 yard 3/8" hot pink dot grosgrain ribbon

1/4 yard 1/8" – 3/8" green ribbon (See specific projects for ribbon leaf treatment.)

Matching threads

Directions

1. Fold ends of hot pink dot grosgrain ribbon to underside at right angles and gather one edge lengthwise to approximately 5" length; knot securely. Adjust gathers evenly.

2. Tuck in one end and wrap ribbon around end (to be center of rose). Tack gathered wrapped center. Continue wrapping gathered edge around center base, tacking every 1/4", to previous row. Continue to end of gathered strip. *Note:* For this size rose, gathered strip will wrap around center approximately three times.

3. Add ribbon leaves or bows as described in specific project.

Twice as Nice Rose Gown

(See Figure 1-12 and Color Pages)

You can dress your little girl in this pretty pink gown when she is expecting company or use it as a soft and cuddly nightie (the 3-D rose is soft enough to sleep on). Either way, your little girl will blossom when wearing this full-length dress.

Materials

Purchased V-neck gown pattern (pattern used here is Sew Little Layette—see Resource List)

1/4 yard solid pink cotton knit

1/8 yard white with pink pin dot cotton knit

1/2 yard pink with white heart print cotton knit

6" white cotton ribbing

Cotton knit rose with one leaf (see instructions earlier)

Scraps of:

    green pin dot fabric

    tear-away interfacing

    fusible webbing

    lightweight iron-on interfacing

1-1/3 yard 1" white flat eyelet lace

1/3 yard 3/8" kelly green grosgrain ribbon

Matching threads

♥ *Note:* Adjust amounts of cotton knit fabrics and ribbing as needed according to pattern size and requirements. Yardages given here will make up to 12-month size.

Directions

1. Prewash all fabrics and lace trim, and lightly press as needed. Cut top bodice front/sleeve and back/sleeve pieces from solid pink cotton knit. Cut long skirt from pink with white heart print cotton knit. Cut two strips 1" x 60" of pin dot cotton knit for flat piping. Following the instructions, cut white ribbing for V-neck and sleeve cuffs.

2. Sew shoulder seams. Fold strip for flat piping in half lengthwise with wrong sides together and stitch to sleeve cuffs and along V-neckline with 1/8" seam allowance. Following the pattern instructions, attach ribbing to sleeve ends and V-neckline, using 1/4" seam allowance. This allows for a 1/4" flat piping trim.

3. Add flat piping to skirt bottom hem as in Step 2. Right sides together, sew white flat eyelet lace to bottom hem with 1/4" seam allowance. Flip eyelet down. Stitch skirt together to make continuous tube. Topstitch eyelet lace along skirt bottom 1/8" from the seam.

4. Stitch green grosgrain ribbon for rose stem one-third distance from left seam on front of skirt, starting at top edge of skirt. Back scrap of green pin dot with lightweight iron-on interfacing and cut two leaves. Fuse one leaf on each side of ribbon stem as shown in Figure 1-12, position tear-away interfacing underneath leaf pieces, and appliqué with narrow-width satin stitch using matching thread; topstitch veins on leaves as shown on the pattern.

5. Gather top edge of skirt and attach to bodice, following the pattern instructions. Make one cotton knit rose and sew to bodice above stem with leaf positioned as in Figure 1-15. Lightly press gown.

Reversible Rose Bib

(See Figure 1-12)

Materials

1/3 yard pink 100% cotton terry

1/3 yard pink with white heart print cotton knit

1/8 yard white with pink pin dot cotton knit

Cotton knit rose with one leaf (see instructions earlier)

Scrap of white Velcro

Directions

1. Prewash terry and cotton knit fabrics; lightly press as needed. Using the pattern in Figure 1-9, cut one each bib from pink terry and pink cotton knit. Cut binding strip 1-1/2" x 60" pin dot cotton knit.

2. With wrong sides together, baste terry and pink heart knit bibs together with 1/8" seam allowance. Using 3/8" seam allowance, sew binding around bib and neck opening continuously, overlapping ends.

3. Sew one cotton knit rose and one leaf. Tack to terry side of bib at right neckline as in the photo.

4. Cut Velcro pieces 1/2" x 3/4" and stitch to top back corners of bib so back corners just overlap. Lightly press.

Rosebud Wrist Rattle

(See Figure 1-12)

Materials

Cotton knit rose with two leaves (see instructions earlier)

2/3 yard 1" pink/white gingham check ribbon

6" piece 3/4" white elastic

2 brass 3/8" jingle bells

Matching threads

Optional: Dental floss

Directions

1. Make one cotton knit rose with two leaves. Before gathering leaf ends, insert a jingle bell into each leaf. Gather leaf ends tightly and stitch leaves to bottom of rose, opposite each other. *Optional:* Use dental floss here for extra secure closure of leaves and leaf attachment to rose.

2. Cut gingham ribbon into two 10" pieces. Pin ribbon pieces together and stitch with a narrow zigzag along 10" sides. Insert elastic in ribbon casing, gather, and sew narrow ends together. Securely tack ribbon bracelet to back of cotton knit rose, with raw edges of seam facing back of rattle. *Optional:* Use dental floss here for extra secure attachment.

Rose Headband

You've seen these darling headbands in boutiques and catalogs. Now you can sew them, quickly and inexpensively. Use measurements in parentheses to make a matching headband for an older sister. Vary the design by using different colors or multi-ribbon bows instead of a 3-D fabric rose.

Materials

1-1/2 (2) yards 3/8" hot pink dot grosgrain ribbon

1/3 yard 1/4" invisible elastic

Cotton knit rose with two leaves (see earlier instructions)

Matching threads

Optional: Dental floss

Directions

Note: Measurements in parentheses are for larger child.

1. Cut ribbon into two 3/4 (1) yard pieces. Pin with wrong sides together and sew pieces together along lengthwise edges with a narrow zigzag.

2. Insert elastic into ribbon casing, gathering ribbon, and sew narrow ends together securely.

3. Make one cotton knit rose with two leaves opposite each other. Sew rose to ribbon headband with raw edges of connecting seam facing back of rose. *Optional:* Use dental floss to attach rose to headband for extra secure stitching.

Ribbon Rose Anklets

(See Figure 1-2)

Materials

Pair white cotton anklets

2 pink dot grosgrain ribbon roses (see instructions earlier)

2/3 yard 3/8" flat white cluny lace

2/3 yard 1/8" green dot satin ribbon

2/3 yard 1/16" white satin ribbon

Matching threads

Optional: Dental floss

Directions

1. Prewash cotton anklets and lace. Cut cluny lace into two 12" pieces. Overlap and stitch top edge of lace to edge of folded anklet cuff with narrow-width zigzag, stretching anklet cuff as you sew. Repeat for other sock.

2. Make two grosgrain ribbon roses. Cut green and white satin ribbons into 12" lengths. Make four-loop bows with each ribbon piece. Tack green bow with white bow on top through center of bows. Sew bows to back of ribbon rose. Repeat for other rose.

3. Sew bow/ribbon roses to outside of folded cuff through one layer only. Repeat for other sock, reversing position of rose.

Ribbon Trim Anklets

(See Figure 1-2)

Materials

Pair white cotton anklets

1 yard 3/8" white with pink heart print satin ribbon

2 pink 1/2" heart buttons

Matching threads

Directions

1. Prewash anklets. Cut ribbon into two 6" pieces and two 12" pieces. Using 12" length of ribbon, overlap and stitch ribbon edge to folded edge of anklet cuff using narrow-width zigzag, stretching cuff as you sew. Repeat for other sock.

2. Tie two bows with 6" ribbon pieces. Sew bow to outside of one layer of folded anklet cuff with pink heart button at center of bow. Repeat for other sock, reversing position of bow. **Optional:** Use dental floss when attaching button/bow to anklet cuff for secure attachment.

Appliquéd Receiving Blanket

(See Figure 1-19)

Most standard purchased receiving blankets are 28"– 30" square. But to add longer life to your blanket, I suggest making a 36" square receiving blanket. The more you wash the blanket, the softer it becomes. And these blankets are perfect for covering a napping toddler when temperatures drop.

Materials

1-1/8 yards cotton double brushed pink flannel

1/8 yard white with pink pin dot cotton knit

4 rose appliqués with leaves

1/8 yard tear-away interfacing

Matching threads

Directions

1. Prewash flannel and cotton knit. Lightly press as needed. Cut flannel into 36" square, rounding all corners evenly.

2. Cut pin dot cotton knit into three 1-1/2" x 60" strips. Stitch narrow ends of strips together to make one long strip. Sew knit binding around outer edge of blanket with 3/8" seam allowance, overlapping ends.

3. Position and fuse rose appliqués to corners of blanket, following placement in the photo. Cut four pieces of tear-away interfacing larger than rose appliqué and pin to wrong side of blanket underneath appliqué areas. Appliqué roses to corners, remove tear-away interfacing, and lightly press.

♥ **Note:** For an extra-special blanket, line blanket with coordinating flannel print fabric. This double-fabric blanket will give years of cuddly service.

Rosebud Burp Pad

(See Figure 1-19 and Color Pages)

Wonder what to do with cotton terry remnants or scraps? Stitch up a stack of burp pads to toss over your shoulder when burping or carrying baby. They're also handy for diaper changes, spills, or other mishaps.

Materials

1/3 yard pink cotton terry or scraps from other projects

1/8 yard white with pink pin dot cotton knit or scraps from other projects

3 rose appliqués (see instructions earlier)

Scrap of tear-away interfacing

Matching threads

Directions

1. Prewash pink terry and cotton knit. Cut rectangle 10" x 20" from pink terry. For binding strips, cut one 1-1/2" x 60" strip from pin dot cotton knit.

2. Round all corners evenly. Bind raw edges with knit strip, using 3/8" seam allowance and overlapping ends.

3. Position and fuse three rose appliqués across narrow bottom end of rectangle. Cut piece of tear-away interfacing larger than appliqué area and pin to wrong side of burp pad underneath appliqués. Appliqué roses, remove tear-away interfacing, and lightly press.

Baby Rosebud Bunting

(See Color Pages)

This charming outerwear is perfect for fall or winter babies, as they keep warm and cozy tucked inside the bunting. Plan to make a bunting for an infant up to six months of age. Snowsuits are a better choice for older tots, offering more mobility. Select double-backed quilted knit or woven cotton fabrics for main garment. To continue theme of garments shown here, choose a small floral print in pastel colors.

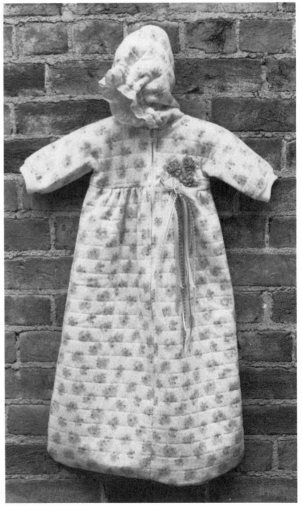

Fig. 1-17

Materials

Purchased bunting pattern (pattern used here is Sew Little Layette—see Resource List)

1 yard pastel floral print, double-backed quilted cotton knit

2/3 yard 1" white flat eyelet lace

1/3 yard 1/4" white elastic

3" white cotton ribbing

1/8 yard white with pink pin dot cotton knit

White 20" zipper

3 hot pink dot grosgrain ribbon roses (see earlier instructions)

1-1/3 yards 1/8" pink dot satin ribbon

2-1/2 yards 3/8" light green satin ribbon

1-1/3 yards 5/8" white sheer stripe picot ribbon

Matching threads

Directions

1. Prewash quilted knit, pin dot knit, ribbing, and lace trim. Cut bunting and hood pieces from floral quilted knit fabric as directed in your purchased pattern. Take care to match quilted lines and floral design during pattern layout. Cut one strip 1-1/2" x 60" white with pink pin dot cotton knit for binding strip, to be used inside the hood.

2. Following the pattern instructions, sew hood with right sides together. With right sides together, baste eyelet lace to hood opening with 1/8" seam allowance. Make casing with pin dot knit binding and 3/8" seam allowance. Insert elastic in casing and tack ends securely. Set hood aside.

3. Assemble bunting following the pattern instructions, using white cotton ribbing for sleeve cuffs. After attaching hood to main bunting, encase seam using pin dot knit binding.

4. Make three grosgrain ribbon roses. Cut nine pieces of light green satin ribbon, each 3" long. Hold ribbon end, twist other end around, and place on top of first end. Tack and gather ends together for ribbon leaf. Make eight more leaves in this manner. Tack three leaves to bottom of each rose as shown in Figure 1-17.

5. Sew roses to one side of bodice as shown in the photo. Cut remaining light green ribbon into two equal pieces. Make one six-loop bow with one light green ribbon piece. Using white sheer stripe picot ribbon, cut one piece 18" long and one piece 21" long for streamers. With remaining 9" piece, make double loop bow. Cut pink dot satin ribbon into one 22" length and one 26" length.

6. For streamers, fold ribbons in half and tack together at fold in this order: two light green ribbons, two white sheer stripe picot ribbons, and two pink dot ribbons. At top of folded streamers, sew light green six-loop bow. Tack white sheer bow through center of bow/streamer frill. Tack multi-bow/streamer frill under ribbon roses along seamline with streamers extending down front of bunting. Lightly press bunting.

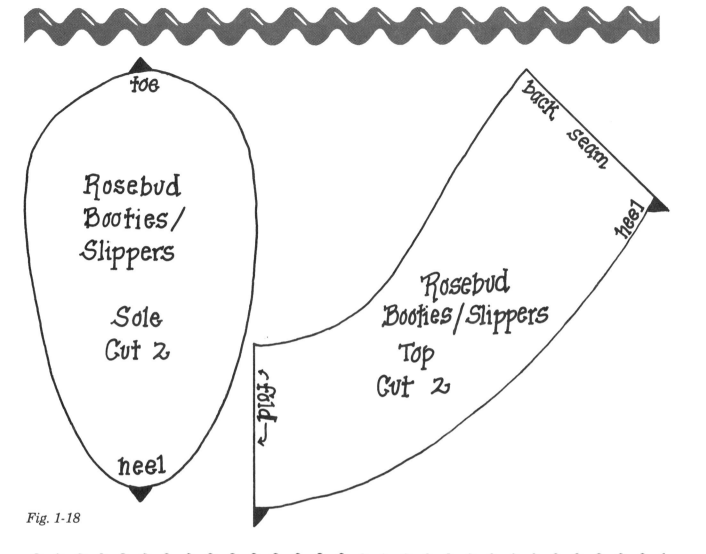

Fig. 1-18

(Pattern labels: toe, heel — Rosebud Booties/Slippers Sole Cut 2; back seam, heel, fold — Rosebud Booties/Slippers Top Cut 2)

Rosebud Booties for the Littlest Ballerina

(See Color Pages)

One of the best advantages of making layette goodies is that the leftover scraps can be coordinated to make accessory items.

Materials

1/4 yard floral pastel print, double-backed quilted cotton knit or scraps from bunting

1/8 yard white with light blue pin dot cotton knit or scraps from boy's layette

2 pink dot grosgrain ribbon roses (see instructions earlier)

1/2 yard 3/8" light green satin ribbon

1-1/3 yards 1/8" pink dot satin ribbon

1-1/3 yards 1/16" white satin ribbon

Blunt needlepoint needle

1/2 yard 1/4" invisible elastic

Matching threads

Directions

1. Prewash quilted knit and cotton knit fabrics. Cut two sole pieces and two top bootie pieces from floral pastel print quilted fabric (see Figure 1-18). Cut binding strip 1" x 60" of pin dot knit.

2. Using 1/8" seam allowance, sew back heel seam with right sides together. Sew a row of hand or machine basting stitches around bottom of top bootie piece. With wrong sides together, pin top bootie to sole, gathering basting stitches to ease in fullness. Baste around sole. Using 1/4" seam allowance, attach knit binding strip around sole and overlap ends.

3. Sew binding strip in same manner around top foot opening of bootie, leaving 1/2" opening at back of heel. Cut two 9" lengths invisible elastic. Thread blunt needlepoint needle with invisible elastic and thread through top binding/casing. Pull elastic to lightly gather opening so bootie will hold onto foot. Knot elastic ends together three to four times, clip ends, and stitch binding/casing closed. Repeat for other bootie.

4. Make two pink dot grosgrain ribbon roses. Cut six 3" pieces of light green ribbon. Make ribbon leaves as in Step 4 of bunting instructions. Attach three leaves to bottom of each rose as shown in Figure 1-17. Sew roses to top toe area of each bootie, with the leaves pointing up.

5. Cut two 1-1/2" pieces of 1/16" white satin ribbon. Make loop of ribbon and tack to inside heel of each bootie for ribbon ties in Step 6. The loop extends slightly above the back heel.

6. Cut pink dot satin ribbon and white satin ribbon into equal length pieces. Take one of each color ribbon and thread through back heel loop. Tie in center. Repeat for other bootie.

7. When baby wears booties, fit bootie on foot, wrap ribbon ties around twice, making an "X" at back of ankle, and tie in bow in front.

Rosebud Straw Hat

(See Figure 1-19 and Color Pages)

We are all aware of how the sun can burn tender baby skin. This sweet sunhat will protect your tot, while setting new standards for style. Natural straw can scratch tender skins; select a softer synthetic weave instead.

Materials

Synthetic straw hat with brim

Cotton knit rose with two leaves (see instructions earlier)

3 yards 1/8" pink dot satin ribbon

3 yards 1/8" green dot satin ribbon

2 yards 1/16" white satin ribbon

Blunt needlepoint needle

Matching threads

Optional: 1 yard 3/8" pink dot ribbon for ties

Directions

1. Cut ribbons into 1-yard lengths. Thread green dot ribbon into needlepoint needle and stitch around outside row closest to edge of brim using a straight stitch. For best results, stitch with 1/2" long stitch on right side of brim and a 1/8" stitch on wrong side. After sewing around brim, end stitches on wrong side and knot. Trim ribbon knot ends.

2. On next straw row in, use same decorative stitches with a row of pink dot satin ribbon. Knot in same manner as above. Repeat another row of decorative stitches with white satin ribbon.

3. At the point where the crown of the hat rises from brim, locate first complete straw row. Using green dot satin ribbon, stitch a row of ribbon stitches in same manner as on brim. End stitches on wrong side and knot. Trim ribbon ends. Add another row of pink dot satin ribbon stitches above green dot ribbon row; knot as above. Repeat this method for white satin ribbon, green dot satin ribbon, and pink dot satin ribbon.

4. Securely sew cotton knit rose on hat crown as shown in Figure 1-19. *Optional:* Add ribbon ties if desired.

♥ *Baby Bath-Time Boutique*

Whether you have an elaborate baby tub, use the kitchen sink, or prefer to give sponge baths, you'll agree that keeping baby clean and sweet-smelling is a daily (sometimes hourly) task. Using the bath-time linens shown here, you can make quick-to-stitch projects that have carriage-trade appeal. When selecting materials for these projects, choose 100% cotton terry and cotton knits for best absorbency and wear. Each set of directions gives instructions for either bunny or rose appliqués.

Fig. 1-19

Set of Four Appliquéd Washcloths

While browsing in bath and baby boutiques to keep up with current trends, I found a four-pack of appliquéd washcloths similar to the ones shown here, retailing for $25.00. The washcloths in this book were made for approximately one-fifth that amount, in an hour's time. The terrycloth has one side with shorter loops than the other. I prefer to fuse the appliqués to the short-looped side.

Materials

1/3 yard white 100% cotton terry, at least 48" wide

1/6 yard white with light blue pin dot cotton knit

4 blue bunny appliqués, two facing left and two facing right (see earlier instructions)

1/8 yard tear-away interfacing

1 yard 5/8" light blue picot ribbon

Matching threads

Directions

1. Prewash terry and cotton knit fabrics. Cut four 11" squares white terry and round all four corners of each washcloth evenly.

2. Cut four strips 1-1/2" x 60" pin dot cotton knit for binding strips.

3. Encase raw edges of washcloths with knit binding strips, with 3/8" seam allowance, overlapping raw edges.

4. Cut four pieces tear-away interfacing slightly larger than bunny appliqués. Position and fuse one bunny appliqué to one corner area of each washcloth. Pin tear-away interfacing to **wrong** side of washcloth underneath appliqué area. Appliqué bunny as in earlier instructions. Remove interfacing. Press lightly.

5. Repeat for other three washcloths. Fold washcloths into quarters and tie together with picot ribbon and bow. Cut ribbon ends at an angle.

Rosebud Washcloths

(See Figure 1-19)

Materials

1/3 yard pink 100% cotton terry, at least 48" wide

1/6 yard white with pink pin dot cotton knit

4 white chintz rose appliqués (see instructions earlier)

1/8 yard tear-away interfacing

1 yard 5/8" white picot ribbon

Matching threads

Directions

1. Follow Steps 1 – 4 on the previous pages, using rosebud material instead of bunny material.

2. Repeat for other three washcloths. Fold washcloths into quarters and tie together with picot ribbon and bow. Cut ribbon ends at an angle.

♥ *Hint:* When laundering washcloths, only use fabric softener every third wash for best terry absorbency.

Bunny Diaper Changing Pad

(See Figure 1-5)

Materials

1/3 yard white 100% cotton terry

1/8 yard white with light blue pin dot cotton knit or scraps from previous projects

2 facing blue bunny appliqués with heart appliqué (see instructions earlier)

Scraps of:

    white with light blue stripe chintz

    6" piece of 1/4" white satin ribbon

1/8 yard tear-away interfacing

Matching threads

Directions

1. Prewash terry and cotton knit fabric. Cut rectangle 12" x 18" of white terry and round all corners evenly. (Set aside leftover terry for mitt.) Cut one strip 1-1/2" x 60" from pin dot cotton knit for binding strip.

2. Bind raw outer edges of changing pad with pin dot strip, using 3/8" seam allowance. Cut one heart appliqué from white chintz scrap (see Figure 1-7). Position and fuse facing bunnies with heart appliqué in center, along 12" side of changing pad, as seen in Figure 1-19.

3. Cut piece of tear-away interfacing 4-1/2" x 12" and pin to wrong side of changing pad **underneath** appliqué area. Satin stitch appliqués. Remove tear-away interfacing; lightly press. Tie bow of 1/4" white satin ribbon and tack securely to heart appliqué to match bows on bunnies.

Rosebud Diaper Changing Pad

Materials

1/3 yard pink 100% cotton terry

1/8 yard white with pink pin dot cotton knit or scraps from previous projects

3 white chintz rose appliqués (see instructions earlier)

1/8 yard tear-away interfacing

Matching threads

Directions

Follow Steps 1 – 3 on previous pages, using rosebud material instead of bunny material. Cut three rose appliqués; position and fuse roses evenly across bottom of pad.

Bunny Wash Mitt

Materials

1/3 yard white 100% cotton terry or scraps from diaper changing pad

1/8 yard white with light blue pin dot cotton knit or scraps from previous projects

1/8 yard tear-away interfacing or scraps from other projects

1/2 yard 1/4" white satin ribbon

1/4 yard 3/8" invisible elastic

Blue bunny appliqué facing right (see instructions earlier)

Matching threads

Directions

1. Prewash terry and cotton knit fabrics. Cut two mitts (see Figure 1-20) from white terry and one strip 1-1/2" x 60" of pin dot cotton knit for binding.

2. Position and fuse bunny to center of one mitt piece for front of mitt. Cut piece of tear-away interfacing slightly larger than appliqué and pin to wrong side of mitt **underneath** bunny appliqué. Stitch bunny appliqué as in earlier instructions. Remove tear-away interfacing and press.

3. With wrong sides together, pin mitts together and stitch from bottom left side to top of mitt with 1/4" seam allowance. Open mitt. On wrong side of mitt, pin, stretch, and zigzag invisible elastic 1-1/4 " above bottom of mitt. Fold mitts together, wrong sides together. Encase sides and top of mitt with knit binding strip using 3/8" seam allowance. Encase bottom raw edge of mitt with binding strip, leaving 6" tie end. Blind stitch tie end, loop, and tack end to bottom right side of mitt.

4. Make four-loop bow of white satin ribbon and tack to bottom right side of mitt where loop is sewn. For gift presentation, add some specialty baby soaps available at pharmacies.

Fig. 1-20

Wash   Mitt

Cut 2

Guide line   for invisible elastic

Rose Wash Mitt

(See Figure 1-19 and Color Pages)

Materials

1/3 yard pink 100% cotton terry or scraps from diaper changing pad

1/8 yard white with pink pin dot cotton knit or scraps from previous projects

1/2 yard 1/4" white satin ribbon

1/4 yard 3/8" invisible elastic

Cotton knit rose with two leaves (see instructions earlier)

Matching threads

Directions

1. Follow Steps 1 – 3 on previous pages, using rose material instead of bunny material.

2. Make four-loop bow of 1/4" white satin ribbon and tack to bottom right side of mitt where loop is sewn. Securely sew cotton knit rose to front of mitt where shown in Figure 1-19. For gift presentation, add some specialty baby soaps available at pharmacies.

Appliquéd Hooded Towel

(See Fig. 1-5)

These essential bath-time towels are worth their weight in gold. Most hooded towels available in baby boutiques are a standard 28" square. But larger babies and toddlers appreciate the cuddly quality of a terry wrap, too.

I suggest making towels at least 30" square to accommodate growth of the child. Should you choose to make one of these towels for a toddler, use the measurements shown in parentheses for a 36" hooded towel. Select a top quality, 100% cotton terry cloth to provide years of service.

Keep in mind that any of the appliqués in this book could be used to embellish the hood.

Materials

1-1/8 (1-1/4) yards light blue 100% cotton terry

1/6 yard white with light blue pin dot cotton knit

2 facing white bunny appliqués (see instructions earlier)

5 white 1/2" ribbon rosebuds (purchased)

1/2 yard 1/8" green with white dot satin ribbon

1/8 yard tear-away interfacing

Matching threads

Directions

Note: Directions for a larger towel are in parentheses.

1. Prewash terry and cotton knit fabrics. Cut a 30" (36") square of light blue terry and round corners evenly for easy edge binding. Cut hood piece as right triangle with two 10" (12") sides from terry scraps. Round right angle corner as with the large square terry piece. Cut three strips 1-1/2" x 60" of the pin dot cotton knit for binding. Stitch narrow ends with right sides together (1/4" seam allowance) for a continuous piece of binding trim.

2. Bind diagonal edge of hood with pin dot knit binding strip using 3/8" seam allowance. Position and fuse two facing white chintz bunnies on hood as shown in Figure 1-5. Cut piece of tear-away interfacing larger than appliqué area and pin to wrong side of hood underneath bunnies. Appliqué bunnies to hood. Remove interfacing and lightly press.

3. Cut 1/8" green ribbon into five equal pieces. Remove ribbon leaves originally on purchased ribbon rosebuds and replace with leaves of green dot ribbon. Securely tack white ribbon rosebuds around bunnies as shown in Figure 1-5.

4. Baste right angle edges of hood to corner of large towel piece, long looped sides together. Sew knit binding around towel's perimeter, overlapping and tacking under ends.

Rosebud Hooded Towel

Use the directions given for the hooded towel, changing the bunny appliqués to a cluster of three appliquéd roses. With white or pink terry and white with pink pin dot cotton binding strips, you'll love the results.

Additional Ideas

To match the bunny bath-time boutique, you can also sew receiving blankets and burp pad as shown in Baby Rosebud Boutique, substituting light blue or white flannel and terry for main project and white with light blue pin dot cotton knit binding strips. Use bunny appliqué instead of rose appliqué.

♥ *Presto Pizzazz— Bear Necessities Boutique*

Using purchased rompers or a simple cardigan sweater, scrap bag fabrics, and trims, you can change an oufit from plain to pizzazz. And each piece can be embellished in less than an hour.

Because the teddy bear appliqué is used to coordinate these projects, separate instructions are given here for this appliqué design.

Fig. 1-21

Fig. 1-22

Bear Appliqué

Materials

1/4 yard cotton, pastel mini-print

1/8 yard lightweight iron-on interfacing

Polyfil stuffing

Cotton lace according to each project's requirements

Matching threads

Directions

1. Prewash all fabrics and cotton lace; press as needed. Back fabric for teddy appliqué with lightweight iron-on interfacing. Cut one bear appliqué (see Figure 1-23) from above fabric and pin in place. Cut a piece of lightweight iron-on interfacing slightly larger than bear appliqué and fuse to wrong side of garment underneath appliqué area.

Fig. 1-23

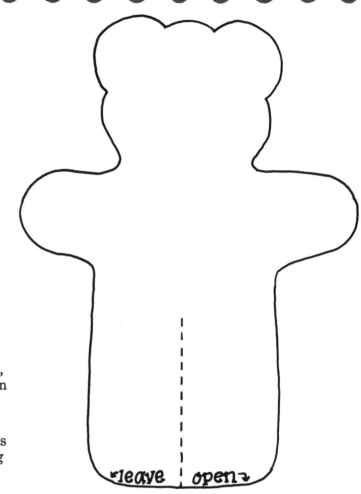

Bear appliqué
for " Bear
Necessities"—
Presto Pizzazz

‹leave ¦ open›

2. Using a medium-width satin stitch, appliqué around bear, leaving open at the bottom as shown on the pattern. Lightly stuff the bear with polyfil and satin stitch bottom edge closed. With a straight stitch, topstitch leg detail as shown on the pattern piece.

3. Embellish bear with trim according to the directions for each project. Trim excess lightweight iron-on interfacing from wrong side of appliqué.

Girl's Romper
(See Color Pages)

Materials
Purchased pink one-piece romper

2/3 yard 3/8" white flat heart lace

1/3 yard 1-1/4" white taffeta picot ribbon

1/8 yard 1" flat white cluny lace

1/4 yard 1/4" light blue satin ribbon

1/4" pink heart button

Matching threads and dental floss or elastic thread

Directions
1. Appliqué bear to romper front as described in the bear appliqué instructions. Ruffle 1" cluny lace and tack to bear at neck. Tie four-loop bow using 1/4" light blue satin ribbon and securely tack pink heart button to center of bow. Sew bow at neckline of bear slightly off-center as shown in Figure 1-22. **Please be sure to securely stitch bow and button in place with either dental floss or elastic thread, as little fingers can be very strong.**

2. Using narrow zigzag stitch, sew heart lace to edge of sleeves, overlapping lace at underarms.

3. Tie bow with white taffeta picot ribbon and tack at neckline using dental floss or elastic thread, slightly off-center to one side. Lightly press romper.

Boy's Romper

(See Color Pages)

Materials

Purchased light blue one-piece terry romper

2/3 yard white jumbo rickrack

7 white 1/4" star buttons

1/8 yard 1/4" light blue satin ribbon

Scrap of 1-1/2" white flat eyelet lace

Matching threads and dental floss or elastic thread

Directions

1. Appliqué bear to romper front as described in the bear appliqué instructions. Cut eyelet bib from eyelet scrap following the pattern guide and appliqué to bear at neck and armholes with a medium-width satin stitch. Tie a double-loop bow using light blue satin ribbon and securely tack star button to center of bow. Sew bow to center top of eyelet bib. **Please be sure to securely stitch bow and button in place with dental floss or elastic thread, as little fingers can be very strong.**

2. Using a narrow zigzag, stitch white jumbo rickrack to edge of sleeve, overlapping and tucking under ends at underarms.

3. Sew white star buttons around neckline as shown on the Color Pages. A good rule of thumb is to sew buttons securely and then to stitch them twice again for extra measure. Lightly press romper.

White Cardigan Sweater

(See Figure 1-21)

Materials

Purchased white acrylic cardigan sweater

1-1/8 to 1-1/2 yards 1/2" white flat lace trim (yardage depends upon sweater size you are making)

5 to 6 white, round 3/8" iridescent pearl buttons (number of buttons depends upon sweater size)

1/4 yard 1/4" pink satin ribbon

White 1/4" pearl heart button

1/8 yard 1" white flat cluny lace

Matching threads and dental floss or elastic thread

Directions

1. Using narrow-width zigzag stitch, sew lace around neckline along bottom edge of ribbing. Straight stitch lace along vertical edge of top overlapping side of sweater; and stitch lace to ends of sleeves. Replace sweater's buttons with pearl buttons.

2. Appliqué bear to left side of sweater. Ruffle leftover piece of lace and tack to bear at neck. Tie four-loop bow using 1/4" pink satin ribbon and securely tack pearl heart button to center of bow. Sew bow at neckline of bear slightly off-center as shown in Figure 1-22. **Please be sure to securely stitch bow and button in place with dental floss or elastic thread, as little fingers can be very strong.**

♥ Sweater Adaptation for Boys ♥

Instead of the following:	Use:
White flat lace trim	Light blue mini-rickrack
Round pearl buttons	White star buttons
Pink mini-print fabric (for bear)	Light blue mini-print (for bear)
Trim detail of bear	Match detail of romper

Teddy Bear Rattle

(See Figure 1-10)

Materials

1/4 yard pastel floral mini-print fabric (45" wide fabric will make two bear rattles)

1/3 yard 1" white flat cluny lace

1/4 yard 1" pink check taffeta ribbon

Pink 3/8" heart button

Small plastic rattle

Polyfil stuffing and batting

Disappearing ink marking pen

Matching threads and dental floss or elastic thread

Directions

1. Trace bear pattern for rattle (Figure 1-24) on typing paper and cut out. Place pattern on wrong side of folded fabric and draw around bear with disappearing ink marking pen. This line is your stitching line. When making several bears, allow 1/2" between bears on fabric.

2. Pin pieces to keep them from shifting, and stitch along drawn line using small straight stitch (15–18 stitches per inch), leaving open at bottom edge of bear. Cut out bear with 1/4" seam allowance, clip curves, and turn right side out. Stuff head and arms with polyfil stuffing. Remove handle from rattle and wrap small scraps of batting around rattle; insert in upper chest of bear. Continue stuffing around rattle and into legs. Hand stitch opening closed. With a straight stitch, topstitch leg detail.

3. Stitch narrow ends of cluny lace together. Hand gather straight edge of lace, slip on bear neck, and pull threads to gather. Adjust gathers evenly and knot securely.

4. Tie double-loop bow with pink check taffeta ribbon and securely tack heart button to center of bow. Sew bow at neckline of bear slightly off center. **Please be sure to securely stitch bow and button in place with dental floss or elastic thread as little fingers can be very strong.**

♥ *Note:* Bear rattle also works well made from terry cloth scraps.

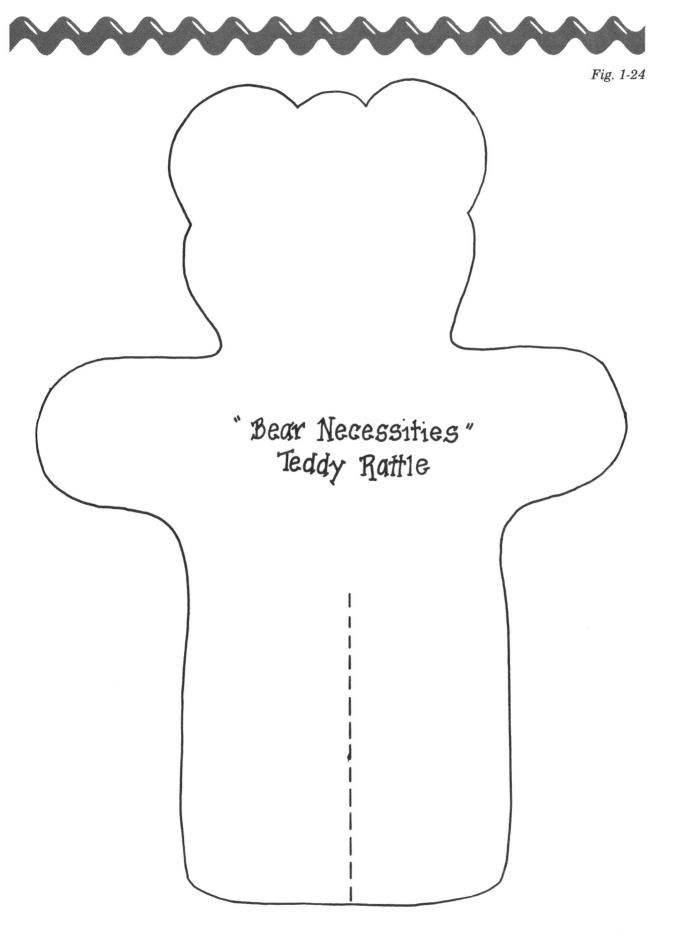

Fig. 1-24

" Bear Necessities "
Teddy Rattle

Pieced and Appliquéd Bib

Fig. 1-25

This project takes a little longer—up to 1-1/2 hours. If you have precut strips of fabric, it saves a lot of time. Use a rotary cutter to cut 1-1/2" wide strips.

Materials

Five coordinating pastel mini-print fabrics in pink, light blue, and white

Scraps of:

    light blue mini-print cotton

    off-white floral mini-print cotton

    1" white flat cluny lace

    polyfil stuffing

Piece of 10" x 12" floral mini-print cotton for bib back

1/4 yard lightweight iron-on interfacing

1 yard 1" white gathered eyelet

3/4 yard 1" pink check taffeta ribbon

1/4 yard 1/4" pink satin ribbon

White 3/8" heart button

Matching threads and dental floss or elastic thread

Directions

1. Prewash all cotton fabrics and lace; press as necessary. Cut rectangle of 6-1/4" x 7-1/2" light blue mini-floral cotton fabric. Using the log cabin piecing technique, with a 1/4" seam allowance, make a border of 1-1/2" strips along each side of mini-floral rectangle and add a final top strip. Round off all corners as shown in Figure 1-25.

2. Appliqué bear to light blue center rectangle. Ruffle 1" white cluny lace and tack to bear at neck. Tie four-loop bow using 1/4" pink satin ribbon and securely tack heart button to center of bow. Sew bow at neckline of bear slightly off center per photo. **Please be sure to securely stitch bow and button in place with dental floss or elastic thread, as little fingers can be very strong.**

3. With right sides together, fold bib in half lengthwise. Using cut-out pattern for neck (Figure 1-26), cut neck opening. Open bib flat. Right sides together, stitch eyelet lace trim around bib perimeter with a 1/4" seam allowance, folding back eyelet edges 1/4" from neckline opening. Do not add trim to neck U area.

4. Cut pink check taffeta ribbon into two equal lengths. With raw edges of the ribbons lined up with the top raw edges of the bib, baste in place at neckline for ties.

5. With right sides together, eyelet and ribbons tucked inside, pin bib to backing fabric and sew around bib with 1/4" seam allowance, leaving open along side for turning. Clip corners and curves, turn right side out, and slip stitch opening closed. Lightly press.

"Bear Necessities" Pieced bib neckline cut out

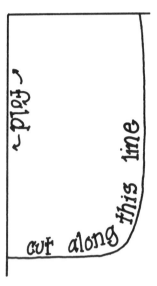

Fig. 1-26

2. *Little Bits Boutique*

Fig. 2-1

Baby showers, church bazaars, or sewing for your own baby: accessories for infants and toddlers are important additions to layettes. All the projects in this section need only one-half yard of fabric or less. Use scrap bag trims to add finishing touches.

In this chapter are directions for a variety of bibs, daisy accessories trio, and tabards for each season.

♥ *Cover-Up Bibs*
This Lil' Piggy
Loch Mess Monster

♥ *Terry Bibs*
Clowning Around
Fairy Godmother

♥ *Fresh as a Daisy Accessory Trio*
Bib
Bonnet
Booties

♥ *Tabards*
Strip Quilted Tabard
Nautical Tabard
Back-to-School
   Apple Tabard
Reindeer Tabard

♥ *Cover-up Bibs*

Once tots are ready for solid foods, they often end up with as much food on them as in their tummies. Make several of these cute cover-ups, with sleeves to protect clothing and with a pocket to catch crumbs.

Keep in mind you can use any of the appliqués and designs in this book to embellish your cover-up bibs. The pattern included here will fit babies up to 25 pounds.

This Lil' Piggy Cover-up Bib

(See Color Pages)

Fig. 2-2

Materials

1/2 yard royal blue Trigger or brushed twill

2/3 yard 1" white gathered eyelet

Package of pink medium-width rickrack

Package of kelly green extra-wide double fold bias tape

3" white cotton ribbing

Squeaker

Scraps of:
    bright pink solid Trigger or brushed twill
    lightweight iron-on interfacing
    fusible webbing
    red and royal blue embroidery floss

Disappearing ink marking pen

Matching threads (pink, green, royal blue, white)

Directions

1. Preshrink royal blue fabric, eyelet, pink scraps, and bias tape trim; press as needed. Trace the bib pattern from Figures 2-4 through 2-6. Cut from royal blue fabric: one front piece, one pocket, two back pieces (one in reverse), and two sleeves (one in reverse). Trace the pig appliqué from Figure 2-3. Back pink fabric with lightweight iron-on interfacing and cut out piggy and large heart appliqué (to be sewn on sleeve). With disappearing ink marking pen, draw in eye and smile with heart cheek on piggy appliqué.

2. Embroider eye with satin stitch and two strands of royal blue embroidery floss. Smile is embroidered with two strands red embroidery floss using stem stitch. Add heart cheek with satin stitch. Cut small heart from royal blue scrap which has been backed with lightweight iron-on interfacing and appliqué to piggy appliqué with contrasting green thread using medium-width satin stitch. Pin piggy to upper part of center bib front piece. Don't use interfacing under the bib because it makes it too hard to insert the squeaker later. Appliqué around piggy with medium-width satin stitch, leaving open between ear and tail. Insert squeaker between bib front and appliqué. Complete satin stitching around piggy. Position, fuse, and appliqué pink heart to upper left sleeve with contrasting green thread using medium-width satin stitch.

3. Trim top edge of pocket with eyelet lace. Sew pink rickrack along bound edge of eyelet lace. Bind top edge of pocket with green bias tape. Pin and baste pocket at sides and bottom to bib front piece with 1/8" seam allowance.

4. Sew raglan sleeves to bib front with right sides together using 1/4" seam allowance. Stitch back pieces to other side of raglan sleeves. Baste eyelet lace trim around neckline with 1/8" seam allowance. Sew pink rickrack along bound edge of eyelet lace. Cut two ribbing cuffs 3" x 6". Fold ribbing in half lengthwise and attach ribbing to sleeve cuffs with 1/4" seam allowance, stretching ribbing to fit sleeve as you stitch ribbing in place. Use a narrow zigzag or stretch stitch. Stitch underarm/side seams, right sides together, using 1/4" seam allowance. Trim entire outer edge of bib with pink rickrack.

5. Starting at top center back edge, stitch green bias tape around bib, starting at top of right back piece, around bib, to top left back piece. Pin-mark center of remaining green bias tape. Pin bias tape center to center front of bib neckline. Complete pinning bias tape around neckline, leaving remaining bias tape ends for ties. Hand stitch neckline binding and ties. Press.

Fig. 2-3

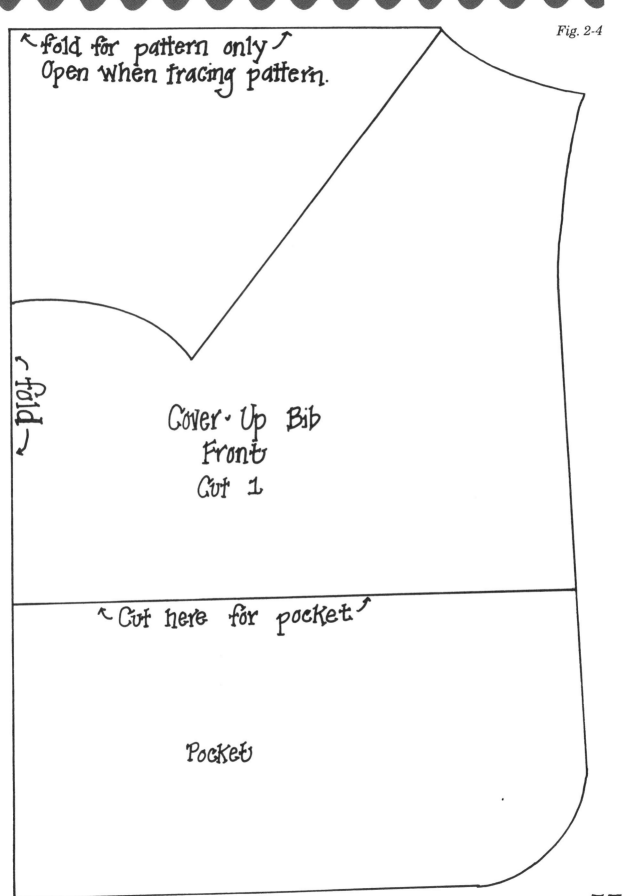

Fig. 2-4

fold for pattern only
Open when tracing pattern.

fold

Cover · Up Bib
Front
Cut 1

Cut here for pocket

Pocket

Fig. 2-5

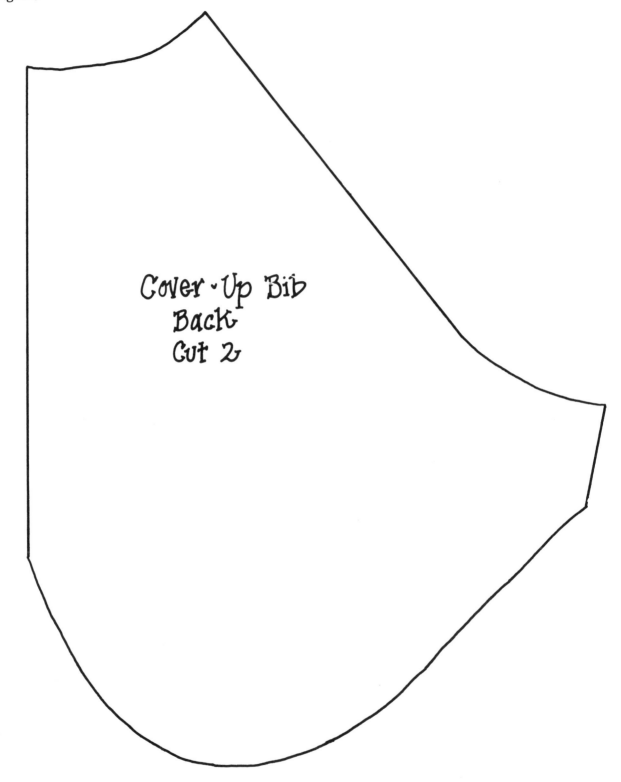

Cover·Up Bib
Back
Cut 2

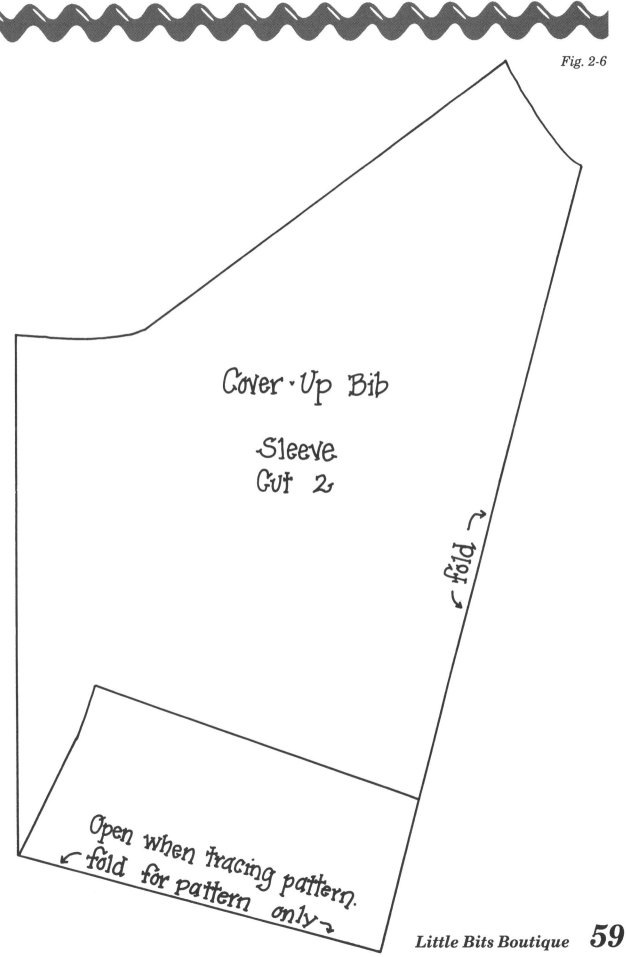

Fig. 2-6

Cover·Up Bib

Sleeve
Cut 2

fold

fold

Open when tracing pattern.
fold for pattern only

Loch Mess Monster Cover-up Bib

(See Color Pages)

Fig. 2-7

Do you have a little messy eater at your house? This bib will amply cover a tot's clothes while dining, yet has sass and style. This appliqué design could also be added to purchased overalls, one-piece jumpsuits, or simple jumper/ dresses.

Materials

1/2 yard tiny yellow gingham check fabric

Package of royal blue double fold bias tape

Package of bright green medium-size rick-rack

1/2 yard orange jumbo-size rickrack

Scraps of:

> green pin dot cotton fabric
> royal blue Trigger or poplin
> lightweight iron-on interfacing
> tear-away interfacing
> fusible webbing
> polyfil stuffing
> white flat heart lace trim

3" white cotton ribbing

Matching threads

Directions

1. Prewash gingham, bias tape, and fabric scraps. Trace the bib pattern in Figure 2-4 to 2-6. For cover-up, cut the following from yellow gingham: one front, two sleeves (one in reverse), two back pieces (one in reverse), and one pocket. Trace appliqué from Figure 2-8. Back green pin dot and royal blue fabric scraps with lightweight iron-on interfacing. Cut out appliqués as follows:

> monster head and tail, green pin dot
> 2 waves, royal blue fabric

2. Position and pin head and tail on upper bib front as shown in the photo. Cut pieces of orange rickrack to fit back spine of head and tail for monster's bumpy spine. Cut small 1/8" wide strips of fusible web, position, and fuse under rickrack to hold in place. Cut pieces of tear-away interfacing larger than appliqués and pin to wrong side of bib front underneath appliqué pieces.

3. To appliqué, set machine for medium-width satin stitch and stitch around head and tail piece of monster, leaving open as shown on the pattern. Stuff a small amount of polyfil to puff out the appliqué. Cut two strips of fusible webbing to fit under wave pieces. Position and fuse over bottom edges of monster's head and tail. Using matching threads and medium-width satin stitch, sew

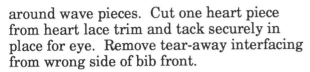

around wave pieces. Cut one heart piece from heart lace trim and tack securely in place for eye. Remove tear-away interfacing from wrong side of bib front.

4. Stitch orange rickrack to top edge of pocket. Trim off 1/4" strip from top edge of pocket. Bind rickrack-trimmed pocket top with royal blue double fold bias tape. Baste pocket to bottom front of bib with 1/8" seam allowance.

5. With right sides together, sew raglan sleeves to bib front using 1/4" seam allowance. In same manner, sew back pieces to sleeve. Cut two white ribbing cuffs 3" x 6". Fold ribbing in half lengthwise and attach ribbing to fit sleeve cuffs, with 1/4" seam allowance, stretching ribbing to fit sleeve end as you stitch. Use a narrow zigzag or stretch stitch. Sew underarm/side seams right sides together with 1/4" seam allowance.

6. Sew green rickrack around bib perimeter, including neckline. Bind raw edge of bib from right center back of bib, around bib, to top of left center back, with royal blue double fold bias tape. Pin-mark center of remaining bias tape. Match pin-mark to center front of neckline. Complete pinning bias tape around neckline, leaving remaining bias tape ends for ties. Hand stitch neckline binding and ties. Tie bias tape ties in knot at ends. Lightly press.

♥ *Hint:* When laundering bib, turn bottom pocket inside out. After laundering bib, lightly press if necessary. Spray with spray starch to help repel stains.

Fig. 2-8

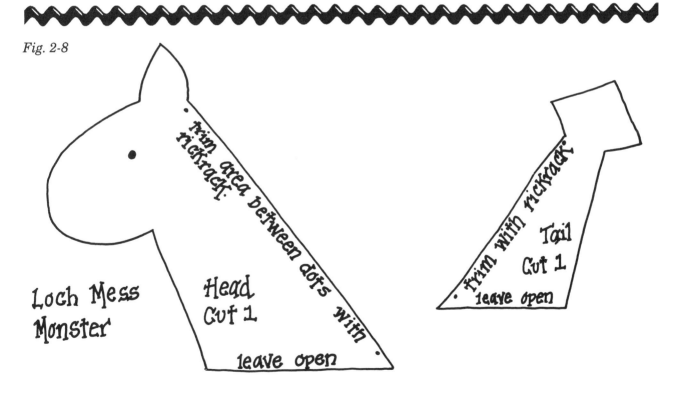

♥ *Terry Bibs*

When you're dealing with drools, drips, and dribbles, terry bibs are the best answer. Using fingertip towels, quick appliqués, and cotton ribbing or ties at the neck, you can stitch a wardrobe of bibs in record time. Each bib uses one fingertip towel. For economy, check linen outlets for discontinued fingertip or hand towels (will make two bibs). Select 100% cotton towels for best absorbency.

If you're making projects for fund raisers or holiday boutiques, these bibs are automatic bestsellers. Any of the appliqués in this book can be used on the bibs. The bibs shown here have embellished edges. Using fingertip towels, you can leave edges plain for quicker projects.

Clowning Around Terry Bib

(See Color Pages)

Fig. 2-9

Materials

Royal blue cotton fingertip towel or hand towel

Package of kelly green extra wide double fold bias tape

Package of red medium-width rickrack

Scraps of:
  unbleached muslin
  green mini-dot cotton
  yellow poplin
  red poplin
  pink mini-print cotton
  red 1/2" fabric flower (purchased)
  lightweight iron-on interfacing
  fusible webbing
  tear-away interfacing
  5/8" rainbow stripe grosgrain ribbon
  royal blue and red embroidery floss

Pink Venus colored pencil

Disappearing ink marking pen

Matching threads

Directions

1. Prewash towel and fabric scraps; press as necessary. Trace the pattern in Figure 2-10. Back fabric scraps with lightweight iron-on interfacing. Cut out appliqué pieces as follows:

> face, unbleached muslin
> hat, green mini-dot
> right and left hair tufts, yellow poplin
> nose, red poplin
> smile, pink mini-print

2. Fold down towel 5-1/2" toward front and cut 5-1/2" diameter semi-circle for neckline through both layers. Trim top folded-over edge and neckline with red rickrack. Bind neckline with kelly green double fold bias tape with 12" ties. Sew red rickrack around edge of front bib, extending up to foldline. Sew kelly green double fold bias tape around towel.

3. Position appliqué on bottom bib. Cut small pieces of fusible webbing and tuck under appliqué pieces; fuse. Tuck 2" piece of red rickrack just under top right side of hat brim. Cut piece of tear-away interfacing slightly larger than appliqué area and pin to underside of bib underneath appliqué area. Appliqué clown with medium-width satin stitch and matching threads. Draw in eyes and smiling mouth with disappearing ink marking pen. Remove tear-away interfacing.

4. Embroider eyes with two strands of royal blue embroidery floss and satin stitch. Embroider smile with two strands of red embroidery floss and stem stitch. Hand stitch rickrack extending from brim. Securely tack red fabric flower to end of rickrack. Tie 6" piece of rainbow stripe ribbon in bow and tack under chin. Lightly shade cheeks with pink Venus colored pencil. Lightly press.

Fig. 2-10

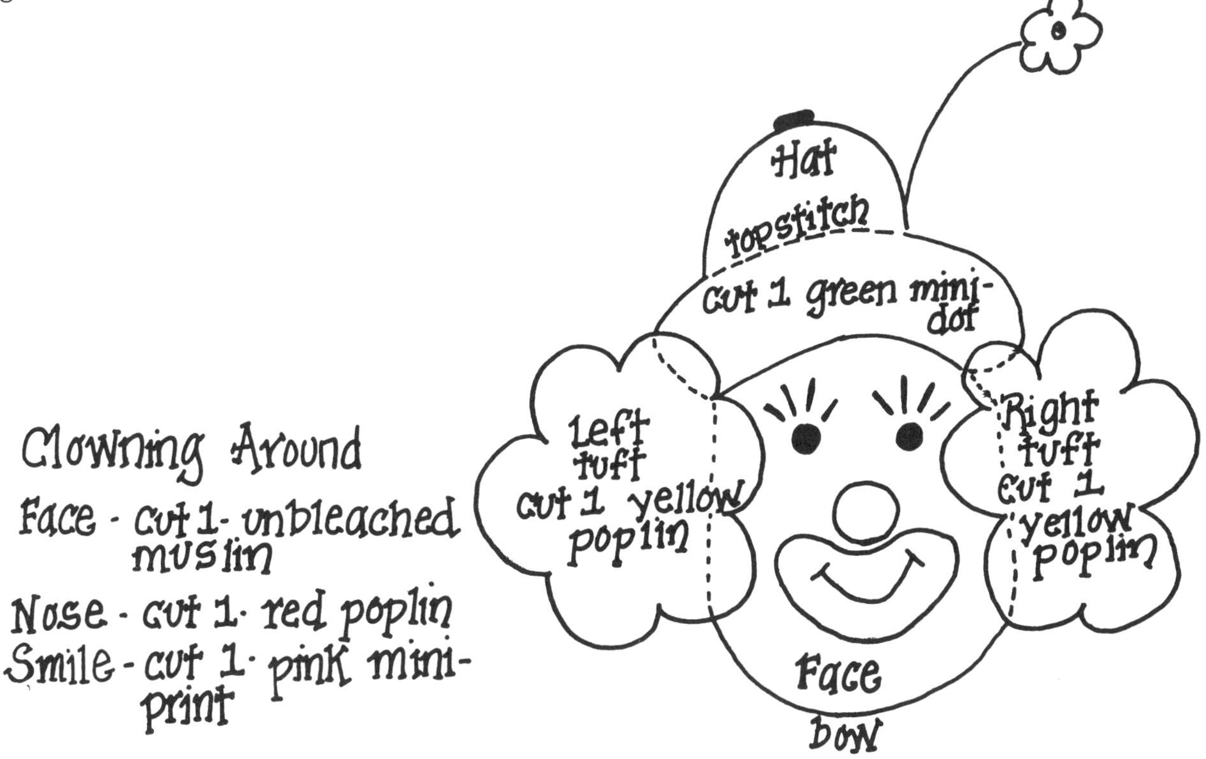

Clowning Around
Face - cut 1- unbleached muslin
Nose - cut 1- red poplin
Smile - cut 1- pink mini-print

Hat topstitch
Cut 1 green mini-dot

Left tuft cut 1 yellow poplin

Right tuft cut 1 yellow poplin

Face

bow

Fairy Godmother Terry Bib

Fig. 2-11

Materials

White cotton fingertip towel or hand towel
1-1/2 yards 1-1/2" white gathered eyelet
6" white cotton ribbing
1/2 yard 3/8" white with pink heart print satin ribbon
1/2 yard 1/16" pink satin ribbon
Scraps of:
    pink mini-heart cotton print
    unbleached muslin
    yellow mini-dot cotton
    white with pink mini-floral cotton
    3/8" white flat lace
    1/8" pink dot satin ribbon
    light blue embroidery floss
    lightweight iron-on interfacing
    tear-away interfacing
    fusible webbing
Gold 10-mm star sequin
Disappearing ink marking pen
Pink Venus colored pencil
Matching threads

Directions

1. Prewash towel and fabric scraps; press as needed. Fold towel down 5-1/2" toward back and cut 5-1/2" diameter semi-circle for neckline opening. Cut white ribbing 6" x 12". Seam 6" sides of ribbing together with 1/4" seam allowance. Fold ribbing tube in half wrong sides together with raw edges even; divide and pin-mark ribbing into quarters. Divide and pin-mark neck opening into quarters. Match up pins for ribbing with neckline opening, with ribbing seam at center back of bib. Sew ribbing to neckline with 1/4" seam allowance, stretching ribbing to fit opening as you stitch. Use a narrow zigzag or stretch stitch. Topstitch around ribbing 1/8" from seam. For lettuce edging, use a medium-width zigzag stitch around the folded edge of the ribbing, stretching ribbing as much as possible as you sew.

2. Trace appliqué pattern from Figure 2-12. Back fabric scraps with lightweight iron-on interfacing and cut out appliqué pieces as follows:

dress, pink mini-heart print
face and hand, unbleached muslin
hair, yellow mini-dot
cap, white with pink mini-floral

3. Position appliqué on bib front. Cut small snips of fusible webbing and tuck under appliqué pieces. Do not fuse pointed end of cap. Fuse appliqués in place. Draw placement for eye, sleeve topstitching, cap topstitching, and lace lines for dress on appliqué pieces with disappearing ink marking pen. Cut a piece of tear-away interfacing slightly larger than appliqué and pin to underside of bib underneath appliqué area. Tuck and pin 3" length of 1/8" pink dot ribbon just under hand for magic wand. Appliqué design with matching threads and medium-width satin stitch—except for pointed end of cap, which should be left open for now. Topstitch sleeve and cap. Sew white flat lace at neckline, sleeve cuff, and wavy line along bottom area of dress. Sew star sequin to end of wand most securely. Embroider eye with two strands of light blue embroidery floss in satin stitch. Shade in cheek with pink Venus colored pencil. Fold 1/16" pink ribbon into 2" loops and tuck under pointed end of cap. Satin stitch around end of cap. Remove tear-away interfacing.

4. Make six-loop bow using white with pink heart print satin ribbon, trimming ends at an angle. Sew bow to right side of neckline as shown in Figure 2-1. Right sides together, trim perimeter of towel with eyelet lace, overlapping ends. Flip lace out and topstitch 1/8" from edge around outside edge of bib. Lightly press.

Fig. 2-12

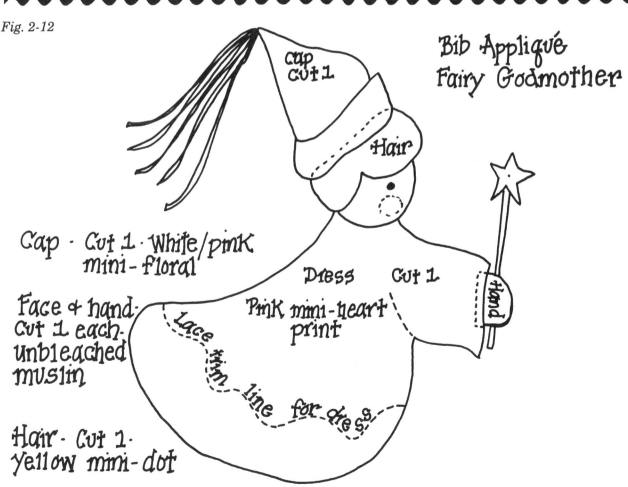

Bib Appliqué
Fairy Godmother

Cap · Cut 1 · White/pink mini-floral

Face & hand· Cut 1 each· unbleached muslin

Hair · Cut 1· yellow mini-dot

♥ *Fresh as a Daisy Accessory Trio*

Fig. 2-13

Whenever I find mini-dot cottons on sale, I stock up. In these daisy accessories, red, green, and navy blue mini-dots combine to create a fresh floral ensemble of bonnet, bib, and booties. One quarter yard of each color will make this treasure trio begin to bloom.

Materials

(For all three projects)

1/4 yard each red, green, and navy blue
    mini-dot cottons
1/4 yard polyfil batting
Package of red double fold bias tape
Package of green medium-width rickrack
2/3 yard 3/8" kelly green grosgrain ribbon
Scraps of:
    white piqué
    lightweight iron-on interfacing
    extra-stiff fusible interfacing
    fusible webbing
    white Velcro (square or circle)
1/4 yard 3/8" white or invisible elastic
5" white cotton ribbing
Matching threads

3-D Daisy Appliqués

Fig. 2-14

Directions

1. Prewash all fabrics; press as necessary. Back 6" x 18" piece of red mini-dot and 4" x 8" piece of green mini-dot with extra-stiff fusible interfacing. Fold pieces in half lengthwise, wrong sides together. Cut fusible web pieces 3" x 18" and 2" x 8", and place between folds of mini-dot pieces. Fuse sandwiched fabrics together securely.

2. Cut five daisies from red mini-dot fused pieces (see Figure 2-14). With red thread and medium-width satin stitch, sew around daisy. Repeat for other flowers. Cut five small leaves from green mini-dot fused fabric. With green thread and narrow-width satin stitch, sew around leaves.

3. Back white piqué with lightweight iron-on interfacing. Cut five daisy centers (see Figure 2-14). Fuse white piqué dots to center of daisies.

4. Position daisy where desired. Tuck leaf end under piqué dot center. Appliqué white piqué daisy center through all thicknesses with medium-width satin stitch and matching thread.

Fig. 2-15

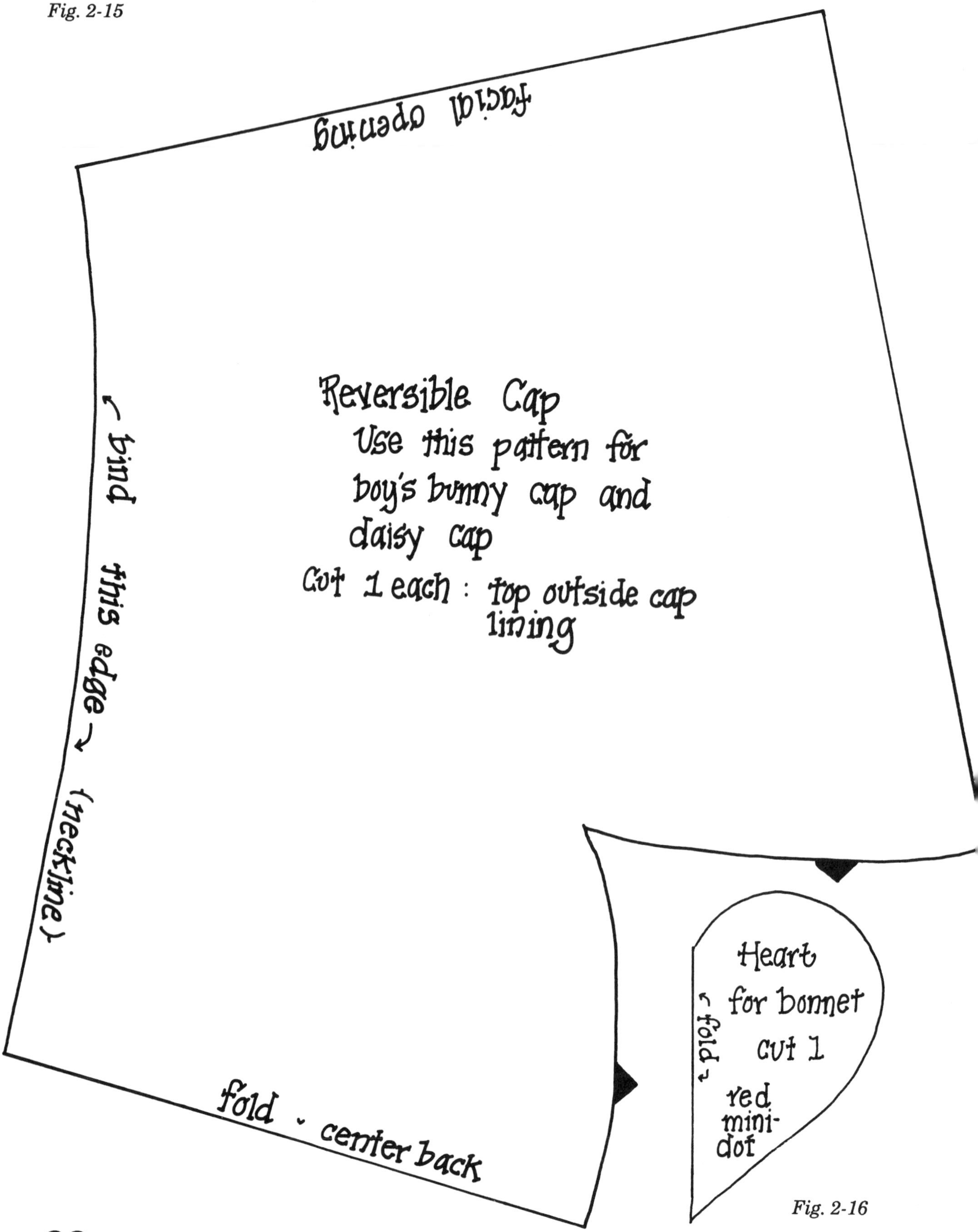

facial opening

← bind this edge → (neckline)

Reversible Cap
   Use this pattern for
   boy's bunny cap and
   daisy cap
Cut 1 each : top outside cap
                    lining

fold · center back

Heart
for bonnet
cut 1
red
mini-
dot

← fold →

Fig. 2-16

Bonnet

(See Figure 2-13 and Covers)

Directions

1. Prewash mini-dot fabrics; press as necessary. Using the pattern in Figure 2-15, cut one each cap from navy mini-dot and green mini-dot. Cut ruffle from red mini-dot 4-1/2" x 32". Back scrap of red mini-dot with lightweight iron-on interfacing and cut out heart appliqué.

2. With right sides together, sew center back seam of navy mini-dot cap, using 1/4" seam allowance. Fold cap for crown seam with center back seam in middle and stitch with same seam allowance. Repeat for green mini-dot cap. Fuse heart appliqué (Figure 2-16) to top of navy cap with medium-width satin stitch. Fold red mini-dot ruffle piece lengthwise with right sides together and sew narrow ends with 1/4" seam allowance. Turn right side out,

matching raw edges. Gather along raw edges to fit facial opening of navy cap, leaving 3/8" unsewn on each side of the navy cap. Right sides together, sew ruffle to navy cap with 1/4" seam allowance. Flip ruffle out. Machine sew green rickrack along seam line of ruffle and hat, tucking under rickrack ends. Pin both caps with right sides together along neckline and stitch with 1/8" seam allowance. Turn so caps fit into each other with navy mini-dot cap on top and wrong sides together. Press. Sew 1/4" seam casing along neckline. Insert elastic into casing and tack ends securely.

3. Fold under facial opening of green mini-dot lining 1/4" and press. Hand stitch to ruffle.

4. Cut green grosgrain ribbon into two 12" pieces for ties. Appliqué daisy centers of two 3-D daisies with small leaves to front neckline corner of each side, tucking ribbon tie end under center of daisy.

Bib

(See Figure 2-13 and Covers)

Directions

1. Prewash mini-dot fabrics; press as needed. In order to fit the pattern in the book, I folded over the pattern. Cut one each of main bib piece (Figure 2-17) from navy mini-dot, green mini-dot, and batting. Cut two daisy bib collar pieces (one in reverse) from red mini-dot (Figure 2-18).

2. Back scrap of green mini-dot with lightweight iron-on interfacing and cut two large leaves and one stem (Figure 2-18). Position and fuse stem down center of navy mini-dot bib, starting at inner neckline. Position and fuse leaves as shown in Figure 2-13 on each side of stem. Appliqué stem and leaves with medium-width satin stitch and matching threads; topstitch leaf veins.

3. Pin red mini-dot scallop collar pieces with right sides together and stitch along scallop edge with 1/8" seam allowance. Clip scallops, turn right side out, and press.

4. Sandwich main bib pieces as follows: green mini-dot right side down, batting, and navy mini-dot right side up. Pin and baste around bib with 1/8" seam allowance. Baste red mini-dot scallop piece around inner neckline with 1/8" seam allowance. Stitch green rickrack starting at the back of the scallops on right side, around bib to back of the scallops on left side. Bind entire perimeter (including inner neckline) with red double fold bias tape, overlapping ends.

5. Appliqué center piqué dot to 3-D daisy appliqué with small leaf at back of bib's right side. Position and sew 1/2" square or circle Velcro pieces so back ends of bib overlap with 3-D daisy side on top. Lightly press.

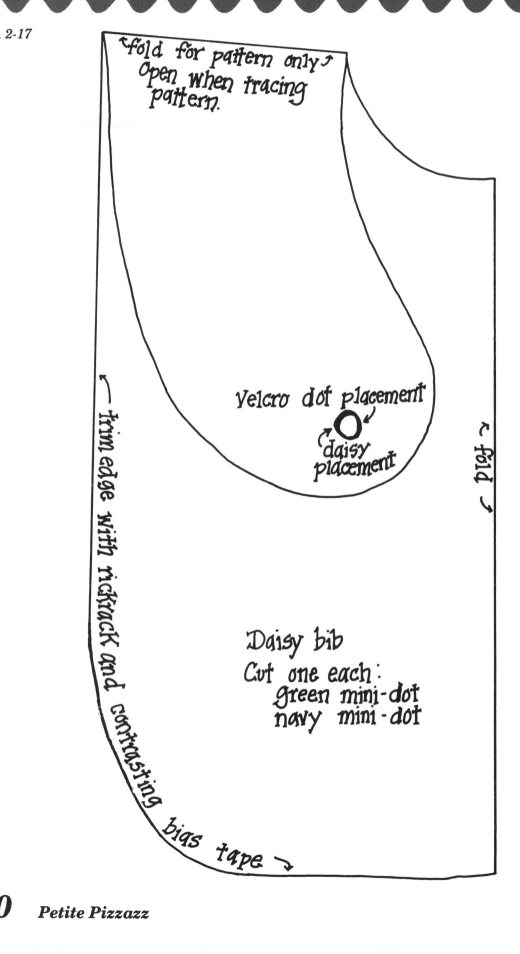

Fig. 2-17

↑fold for pattern only↑
Open when tracing
pattern.

Velcro dot placement

↗
daisy
placement

← fold →

← trim edge with rickrack and contrasting bias tape →

Daisy bib
Cut one each:
   green mini-dot
   navy mini-dot

Fig. 2-18

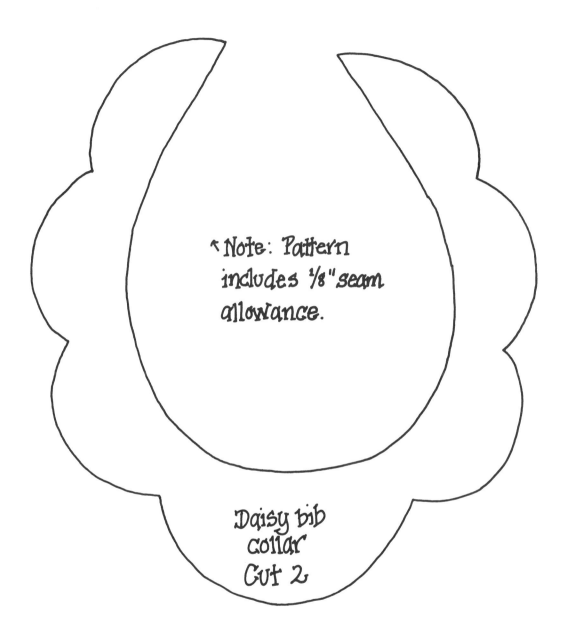

↖Note: Pattern
includes ⅛"seam
allowance.

Daisy bib
collar
Cut 2

large
leaf
appliqué
cut 2
green
mini-
dot

↖top stitch↘

cut 1 · stem – green mini-dot

Booties

(See Figure 2-13 and Covers)

Directions

1. Prewash navy mini-dot fabric and white ribbing. Trace pattern from Figure 2-19. Cut two bootie soles and two bootie tops of navy mini-dot. Cut two white ribbing pieces 4" x 6".

2. With right sides together, sew back seam for bootie tops. Run a row of hand or machine basting stitches 1/8" from bottom edge of bootie top. Pin top bootie piece bottom edge to outer edge of sole with right sides together, gathering basting stitches as necessary to ease. Sew bootie top to sole with 1/4" seam allowance and overcast raw edges. Repeat for other bootie.

3. Sew narrow ends of ribbing together for bootie ribbing. Fold tube in half, wrong sides together, with raw ends together and pin-mark in quarters. Divide top opening of booties into four equal sections. Match up ribbing to bootie top with ribbing seam against back of heel. Sew ribbing to bootie with a narrow zigzag, stretching ribbing to fit as you stitch. Overcast seam.

4. For lettuce edging, stitch with medium-width zigzag along top folded edge of ribbing, stretching ribbing as much as possible as you stitch. Sew 3-D daisy to ribbing cuff on outside edge by appliquéing white piqué center to cuff. Repeat for other bootie. Lightly press.

Fig. 2-19

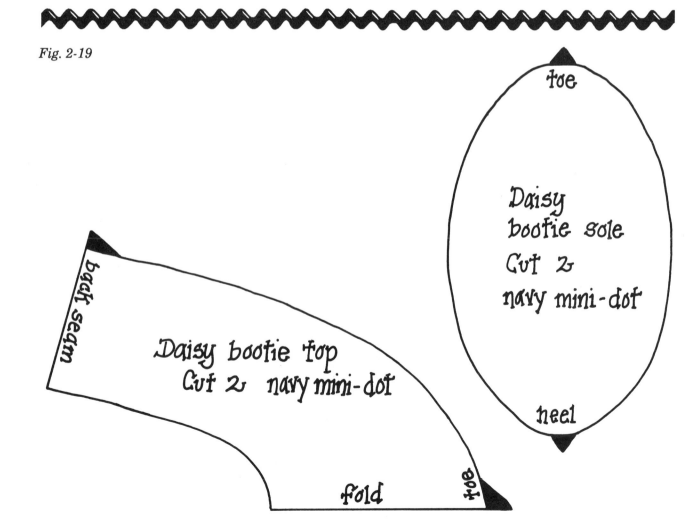

♥ A Tabard for All Seasons

Fig. 2-20

Here's the scenario: The washing machine broke down last week and the repair person won't be able to get to you until tomorrow. The phone rings and it's Aunt Edith—your wonderful, rich, great aunt who hasn't had the chance to see your darling, eight-month old baby. She's at the airport between flights and would dearly love to see you and the little sweetheart.

Gulp! You race to the baby's dresser, and lo and behold, there is one clean stretchie left. You wanted the baby to look extra special for your aunt. What to do?

Tiny tot tabards to the rescue! These little gems use only 1/4 yard of fabric, and can be appliquéd, strip quilted, and

trimmed to your heart's desire. They dress up any outfit to make your baby or toddler look like a million-dollar munchkin. Better than a bib, they top off stretchies, jumpers, overalls, or pajamas to show your offspring has petite pizzazz.

Tiny tot tabards make wonderful baby gifts. The four variations of tabards in this book follow the seasons; you can adapt them to complement both boys' and girls' apparel. Based on the style you select, a tabard can be done in an hour to an afternoon. The list for materials will make both the six- and twelve-month sizes. Use the sizing guidelines in the general information section for help in selecting the correct size to make.

Spring—Strip Quilted Tabard

(See Figure 2-20)

Materials

1/8 yard each of five coordinating pastel mini-prints in the colors of off-white, pink, light blue, and green

1/4 yard coordinating pastel mini-print or solid for lining

1/4 yard polyfil batting

1-1/2 yards 1-1/2" off-white gathered eyelet

Package off-white single fold bias tape

2-1/3 yards 3/8" off-white with pink heart print satin ribbon

1 yard 3/4" off-white flat pointed lace

Scraps of:

    light blue medium-size rickrack

    green mini-rickrack

    off-white flat eyelet trim

Matching threads

Adaptation for boys

Strip quilt assorted plaid, stripe, and dot fabrics. Trim neckline and outside edges with rickrack or piping. Use solid or plaid ribbons for side ties.

Directions

Note: Use 1/4" seam allowance unless otherwise noted.

1. Prewash fabrics and press as needed. While the diagram in Figure 2-21 says to cut two right sides, you will cut one tabard from print for back piece and two tabards each from lining fabric and batting. Cut five print fabrics for strip quilting in strips 1-1/2" x 9". Starting with center front strip, add strips right sides together to each side with flat eyelet lace sandwiched in middle. Sew with 1/4" seam allowance over batting. Flip strips and eyelet out and smooth into place. Keep adding strips to each side, right sides together, using trims in between layers and 1/4" seam allowance. Topstitch seam to make rickrack and/or lace lie flat. Press.

2. Lay back tabard on batting. Pin strip-quilted front tabard to back piece/batting at shoulders, right sides together. Sew shoulder seams. Repeat for lining. Right sides together, baste pointed lace trim around inner neckline of tabard with 1/8" seam allowance. Right sides together, baste gathered eyelet lace and single fold bias tape around outside perimeter of tabard, overlapping and folding back ends. With right sides of lining and tabard together, pin inner neckline and sew with 1/4" seam allowance. Clip corners, turn right side out, and topstitch 1/8" from edge. Press.

3. Fold bias tape to lining and pin. Hand or machine sew bias tape to lining. Press.

4. Cut four pieces of 12" long off-white with pink heart print satin ribbon and tack to lining at sides opposite each other for ties. From remaining heart print ribbon, cut four 9" lengths and tie into bows. Trim bow ends at an angle. Tack bows to neckline corners. Press.

Fig. 2-21

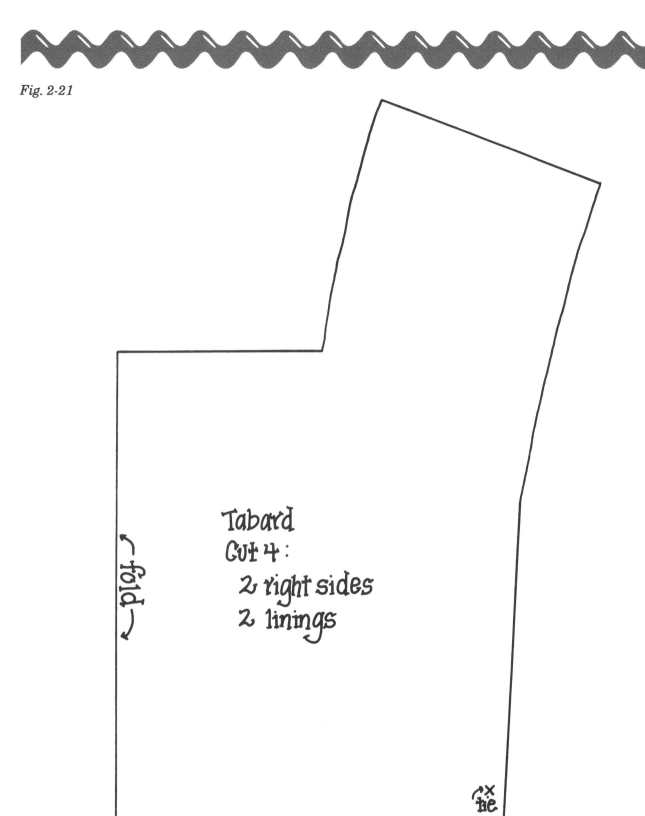

Tabard
Cut 4:
2 right sides
2 linings

fold

x
tie

Summer—
Nautical Tabard

(See Figure 2-20 and Color Pages)

Materials

1/4 yard blue/white pinfeather fabric

1/4 yard white poplin or sailcloth

Scraps of:

    red/white mini-stripe cotton

    lightweight iron-on interfacing

    Aleene's Hot Stitch Fusible Web

    3/4" red dot grosgrain ribbon

Package red piping

1-1/3 yards 3/8" navy dot grosgrain ribbon

2 gold 5/8" star buttons

Matching threads

Fig. 2-22

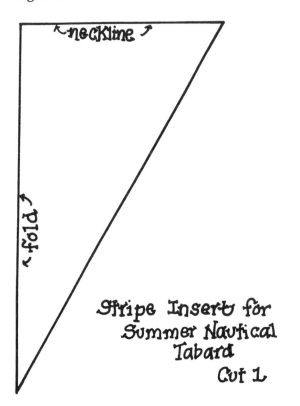

Directions

Note: Use 1/4" seam allowance unless otherwise noted.

1. Prewash fabrics; press as needed. Cut two each (front and back) tabards (Figure 2-21) from blue/white pinfeather and white sailcloth for lining. Back red/white mini-stripe first with lightweight iron-on interfacing and then with Aleene's Hot Stitch Fusible Web. Cut one triangle dickey piece (Figure 2-22) in red/white mini-stripe with stripes running horizontally. Peel off paper backing from dickey, position, and fuse to pinfeather piece at neckline. Appliqué with medium-width satin stitch and matching thread.

2. Pin tabards at shoulders with right sides together and sew shoulder seams separately for tabard and for lining. Press shoulder seams open. Baste red piping around neckline and outer edge of tabard with 1/8" seam allowance. Pin tabard and lining, right sides together, around neckline and stitch with 1/4" seam allowance. Clip corners, turn right side out, and press.

3. Fold under lining along perimeter 1/4" and press. Press piping on pinfeather top for edging. Pin folded edge of lining to piping edging on lining side. Cut four 12" pieces navy dot ribbon ties, insert, and pin to sides opposite each other. Hand or machine stitch lining to piping edging. Cut ribbon ties at an angle. Sew star buttons just below front shoulder seams as shown in Figure 2-20. Tie red dot grosgrain in center, trimming ends in V, and tack to bottom point of dickey. Press.

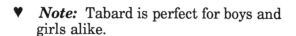

♥ *Note:* Tabard is perfect for boys and girls alike.

Autumn—Back-to-School Apple Tabard

(See Figure 2-20 and Color Pages)

Materials

1/4 yard navy mini-dot cotton
1/4 yard red mini-dot cotton
1/4 yard polyfil batting
Package of dark green single fold bias tape
1-1/4 yards 1" white gathered eyelet
1-1/3 yards 5/8" red grosgrain ribbon
3/4 yard red medium-size rickrack
Scraps of:
    dark green mini-dot cotton
    brown mini-dot cotton
    white with red mini-dot cotton
    lightweight iron-on interfacing
    Aleene's Hot Stitch Fusible Web
Disappearing ink marking pen
Matching threads

Directions

Note: Use 1/4" seam allowance unless otherwise noted.

1. Prewash all fabrics; press as necessary. Cut two each (front and back) tabards (Figure 2-21) from navy mini-dot, red mini-dot, and batting.

2. The back side of this tabard shows an apple core. Back red dot, green dot, brown dot, and white with red dot fabric scraps, first with lightweight iron-on interfacing and then with Aleene's Hot Stitch Fusible Web. Cut out appliqués as follows (Figure 2-23):

    3 apples, red mini-dot
    1 apple top and bottom, red mini-dot
    1 apple core, white with red dot
    3 apple leaves and 1 core leaf, green mini-dot
    3 apple stems and 1 core stem, brown mini-dot

3. Peel off paper backing from appliqué pieces and position three apples evenly across front of navy mini-dot tabard; fuse in place for front. Cut a piece of lightweight iron-on interfacing larger than appliqué area and fuse to wrong side underneath apple appliqués. Appliqué apples, stems, and leaves with matching threads and medium-width satin stitch. With disappearing ink marking pen, draw in comma shapes in upper right portion of apples for "shine." Topstitch "shine" with medium-width satin stitch and white thread. Press.

4. Peel off paper backing from apple core pieces, position, and fuse to lower right side of navy mini-dot tabard back. Cut a piece of lightweight iron-on interfacing and fuse to wrong side of tabard back underneath appliqué. With matching threads and narrow-width satin stitch, sew appliqué. Press.

5. With right sides together, pin and stitch shoulder seams of navy dot tabard. Repeat for lining and batting separately. Press open seams. Sew red rickrack around inner neckline of navy dot tabard with 1/8" seam allowance. Right sides together, trim perimeter of navy dot tabard with eyelet lace, overlapping and folding back ends. Sew dark green bias tape around outer edge over bias binding of eyelet with 1/4" seam allowance.

Back-to-School Tabard

Fig. 2-23

6. Trim 1/4" from outside perimeter of tabard batting. Layer pieces as follows: batting, red mini-dot lining right side up, and navy mini-dot appliquéd tabard right side down. Pin neckline and sew with 1/4" seam allowance. Clip corners, turn right side out, press, and topstitch 1/8" from edge of neckline. Fold under 1/4" around tabard lining and press. Press bias tape to lining side, pin, and sew in place to lining. For ribbon ties, cut four 12" red grosgrain ribbon pieces, pin, and stitch ties opposite each other. Cut ribbon tie ends at an angle. Press.

Variation for Boys

Trim neckline and outer edge of tabard with red or green rickrack or piping.

Winter— Reindeer Tabard

(See Figure 2-20)

Materials

1/4 yard quilted red/green plaid fabric
1/4 yard red poplin or sailcloth
Scraps of:
    tan velour
    tan with brown mini-dot cotton
    red mini-dot cotton
    red holly mini-print cotton
    black and red embroidery floss
    3/8" red bow print satin ribbon
    extra-stiff fusible interfacing
    lightweight iron-on interfacing
    fusible webbing
Brass jingle bell
3/4 yard green piping
1-1/4 yards green jumbo rickrack
1-1/3 yards 5/8" red taffeta picot ribbon
Disappearing ink marking pen
Matching threads and dental floss or elastic thread

Directions

Note: Use 1/4" seam allowance unless otherwise noted.

1. Prewash all fabrics; press as needed. Cut two each (front and back) tabards (Figure 2-21) from plaid quilted fabric and red sailcloth for lining.

2. Back tan velour, red mini-dot, and tan with brown mini-dot fabric with lightweight iron-on interfacing. Cut out appliqués as follows (Figure 2-24):

    reindeer head, tan velour
    muzzle, tan with brown mini-dot
    nose, red mini-dot

Fuse extra-stiff fusible interfacing to back of red holly mini-print piece 5" x 7". Fold piece in half lengthwise with wrong sides together. Cut a piece of fusible webbing 2-1/2" x 7" and sandwich between folded red holly mini-print piece; fuse securely. Cut out antlers from fused holly print. Use red thread and a medium-width to satin stitch antlers alone for 3-D effect; press.

3. Position and fuse reindeer face appliqué to front quilted plaid tabard with 3-D antlers tucked in at top of head as shown in Figure 2-20. With disappearing ink marking pen, draw in eyes, eyebrows, and mouth. Appliqué reindeer face and muzzle with matching threads and medium-width satin stitch. Appliqué nose with narrow-width satin stitch. Embroider eyes and eyebrows with two strands of black embroidery floss and a satin stitch. Embroider mouth with two strands of red embroidery floss in stem stitch. Pin antlers toward bottom of tabard front so they won't be caught in stitching.

4. With right sides together, separately pin and stitch shoulder seams of plaid tabard and of red lining; press seams open. Trim inner neckline of plaid tabard with green piping with 1/8" seam allowance. With right sides together, pin neckline of plaid and lining pieces and stitch neckline seam with 1/4" seam allowance. Clip corners, turn right side out, and press. ***Optional:*** Topstitch 1/8" from edge of inner neckline.

5. Sew green jumbo rickrack around outside edge of plaid tabard. Cut four 12" pieces of red picot ribbon and pin to sides opposite each other for ties. Fold under rickrack so just one set of peaks shows, press, and topstitch on plaid piece 1/8" from edge. Fold under outer edge of lining 1/4" and press. Pin lining to tabard front and hand or machine stitch around tabard. Cut ribbon ties at an angle. Tie a small bow using red bow print ribbon. Securely sew bell to under reindeer's chin with dental floss or elastic thread. Sew bow directly above bell. Press.

Fig. 2-24

Winter - Reindeer Tabard

Part 2

♥ *Puttin' on the Pizzazz—* ♥
A Wardrobe for All Seasons
(for sizes 2 – 8)

3. *Spring Showers*

Among the first sayings I remember learning were "April showers bring May flowers" and "It's raining cats and dogs." Those whimsical sayings triggered my imagination to create this spring ensemble, sturdy enough to withstand muddy spatters, primed with pizzazz for the style-conscious. Starting with everyday denim jumpers and overalls, you can create fashion statements with touches of appliqué and trims. Inexpensive canvas shoes are treated to makeovers, too.

When making jumpers or overalls for children under the age of three, please securely attach all buttons and bells with double strands of dental floss sewn most securely.

In this chapter you'll find directions for charming appliquéd overalls and denim jumper, complete with matching shoes, as well as an embellished rain slicker, hat, and umbrella.

Fig. 3-1

♥ *Darling Doggy*
Overalls
Matching Shoes

♥ *Clever Kitty*
Jeans Jumper
Matching Shoes

♥ *Raining Cats and Dogs*
Slicker
Hat
Umbrella

♥ *Darling Doggy*

Fig. 3-2

Overalls

(See Figure 3-1 and Color Pages)

♥ *Note:* Measurements for rickrack and red gingham ribbon are correct for up to child's size 8. Increase yardage for larger sizes. Overalls shown were manufactured by Oshkosh B'Gosh. For best results, prewash overalls. Remove front bib pocket before starting to embellish overalls.

Materials

Pair of purchased denim overalls
3-1/2 yards red medium-size rickrack
3 yards 3/8" red gingham ribbon
1/2 yard 1/8" green satin ribbon
Scraps of:
    white piqué
    black mini-dot fabric
    gray mini-print fabric
    red mini-plaid fabric
    lightweight iron-on interfacing
    fusible webbing
2 tiny black beads
8 white 1/4" star buttons
2 red 1-1/4" star buttons (for back of overall straps)
Acrylic paints in black and red
0000 fine-line sable paintbrush
Disappearing ink marking pen
Matching threads

Fig. 3-3

Add ribbon loops here

Doggy face for shoes, raincoat and umbrella

Kerchief for doggy face

Darling Doggy Overalls Appliqué

Kerchief for Overalls Appliqué

Directions

1. Back top three fabric scraps listed with lightweight iron-on interfacing and cut out appliqués as follows (Figure 3-3):

> top hair and body/feet, white piqué
> right and left ear, black mini-dot fabric
> main body piece, gray mini-print fabric

2. Position and fuse pieces to overall bib as shown in Figure 3-2. Sew appliqué with medium-width satin stitch and matching threads in the following order: top hair, body/feet, main body, left ear, and right ear.

3. Stitch tiny black beads securely in place for eyes. Draw in face with disappearing ink marking pen and paint as shown in Figure 3-3. Allow paint to dry completely.

4. Cut kerchief from red mini-plaid fabric. Turn under edges 1/4" and hem. Starting to your right side above top of white piqué body, tack kerchief to appliqué, pleating and tacking to fit neck, with tie end to extend to your right as shown in Figure 3-2. Make 1"

to 1-1/2" continuous loops of 1/8" green satin ribbon and tack to bottom of bib for grass as shown in Figure 3-2.

5. Remove suspender hook from right strap and press. Center and stitch red gingham ribbon from right back body of overalls to end of right strap, using a straight stitch on each side of the ribbon. Put hardware back on strap. If you are having problems, refer to buckle on other side. Repeat for left side. Stitch large red star buttons to back where strap joins body.

6. Hand stitch red rickrack around right front pocket, up across bib, and back around left front pocket. Machine sew red gingham ribbon across waistband. Evenly space and tack four white star buttons to front right pocket as shown in Figure 3-1; repeat for left pocket.

7. Baste and machine stitch red gingham ribbon around leg cuff 2" from bottom of leg. Machine sew red rickrack 1/4" above and below gingham ribbon, around cuff. Repeat for other leg.

Shoes

(See Figure 3-1)

♥ *Note:* Measurement for rickrack is accurate up to child's shoe size 13. Increase yardage for larger sizes.

♥ *Equipment suggested:* Needle-nose pliers, clothespins, and Scotchguard spray

♥ *Note:* When making shoes for children under 3, use double strand dental floss to secure buttons in place for shoes.

Materials

Pair of navy canvas slip-on shoes
2 yards red medium-size rickrack
2 yards 1/16" white satin ribbon
16 white 1/4" star buttons
Scraps of:
> white piqué
> black mini-dot fabric
> red mini-plaid fabric

Package Aleene's Hot Stitch Fusible Web Appliqué Pack
Acrylic paints in black and red
Bottle white Slick paint by Tulip Productions
0000 fine-line sable paintbrush
Pink Venus colored pencil
Disappearing ink marking pen
Aleene's Tacky Glue
Matching threads

Clever Kitty Jeans Jumper with Shoes; (close-up) Darling Doggy Overalls (Chapter 3)

(far left) Lighthouse
Scene Sweater,
Nautical Overalls
(Chapter 5), Summer
Nautical Tabard
(Chapter 2); (close-up)
First Mate Sweatshirt
(Chapter 5)

(left) Skibear Thermal
Undies (Chapter 6)

(below) Girl's and
Boy's Velveteen Jumper
and Shortall with
Tabards (Chapter 6)

Patchwork Pizzazz Jumper with Sneakers (Chapter 4)

Directions

1. Trim around shoe opening with red medium-size rickrack using one of these methods: gluing—use clothespins to hold rickrack in place while glue dries; or hand sewing—use strong double thread. Needle-nose pliers make it easier to pull needle through heavy canvas. Using pliers, snip off backs of 1/4" white star buttons and glue to back of each shoe where rickrack overlaps, with three buttons evenly spaced on each side of rickrack trim.

2. Following Aleene's Hot Stitch Fusible Web instructions, fuse to back of piqué and black mini-dot fabrics. Cut two white piqué heads and four black mini-dot ears (two in reverse)(Figure 3-3). Stuff shoe firmly with towel or scrap fabric. Do not use plastic bags as the heat from fusing can melt the plastic in shoe. Fuse head and ears to shoe front following pattern. *Hint:* Do not have iron filled with water when fusing appliqué to shoe front, as hot water can spill on you when you tilt the iron to securely fuse the appliqué. Also take care not to have iron

touch the rubber rim of shoe as it can melt the rubber. Using white Slick paint, paint around edge of face and ears. This method prevents fabric from fraying and also acts as an additional bond to shoe. Wrap 1/16" white satin ribbon around two fingers six times, slip off, and tie in center. Fold loops in V at tie point and glue to top of dog's head for fluffy hair. Repeat for other shoe.

3. Draw in face with disappearing ink marking pen and paint as shown in Figure 3-3. Lightly shade cheeks with pink Venus colored pencil. Allow to dry completely. Cut kerchief from red mini-plaid fabric, turn under edges 1/4", and hem. Starting at your right, tack kerchief to appliqué and shoe, pleating and tacking to fit neck, with tie end to extend to outside of shoe as shown in Figure 3-3. If you have any trouble pulling the needle through, use pliers. Tack or glue small 1/4" star button to "knot" of kerchief. Repeat for other shoe, reversing the direction of the kerchief.

4. To help shoes remain in good condition, spray with Scotchguard spray and repeat as needed.

♥ *Clever Kitty*

Fig. 3-4

Jeans Jumper

(See Figure 3-1 and Color Pages)

Materials

Purchased jeans jumper

2 yards red jumbo rickrack

1-1/2 yards red narrow rickrack

3-1/2 yards 5/8" navy/red/white stripe
    grosgrain ribbon

Scraps of:

    white piqué

    red mini-print fabric

    navy mini-plaid fabric

    1/8" red satin ribbon or red bow button

    lightweight iron-on interfacing

    fusible webbing

Brass 1/4" jingle bell

6 red 1/4" heart buttons

6 white 1/4" star buttons

Acrylic paints in black and red

0000 fine-line sable paintbrush

Disappearing ink marking pen

Pink Venus colored pencil

Matching threads

Directions

1. Back white piqué and red mini-print fabric with lightweight iron-on interfacing and cut out appliqué pieces (Figure 3-5): one cat from white piqué and large heart from red mini-print.

2. Fuse heart to front of jumper bib. Be careful not to position heart too high or you'll have difficulty sewing near buttons. Appliqué heart with matching threads and medium-width satin stitch. Fuse cat piece slightly off-center to left with bottom of cat just reaching waistband. Appliqué with narrow-width satin stitch and matching thread.

3. Draw in face with disappearing ink marking pen and paint as shown in Figure 3-5. Allow to dry completely. Lightly shade cheeks and inner ears with pink Venus colored pencil. Cut kerchief from navy mini-plaid fabric. Turn under edges 1/4" and

hem. Starting at your left, tack kerchief to appliqué at neck, pleating and tacking to fit neck, with tie end to extend to your right as in the drawing. Securely tack jingle bell button to "knot" of kerchief. Tie small bow with 1/8" red satin ribbon (or use red bow button), and tack just above bell.

4. If necessary, remove suspender hook from right strap and press. Center jumbo rickrack on strap; then center and stitch navy/red/white stripe grosgrain ribbon on top of that. Stitch the length of the strap on both sides of the ribbon with a straight stitch. Put hardware back on strap. If you are having problems, refer to buckle on other side. Repeat for left side.

5. Stitch narrow red rickrack across top of waistband and around perimeter of bib including the side opening area. Sew stripe grosgrain ribbon at waistband, so peaks of rickrack just show. Tie two bows with stripe grosgrain ribbon and tack at each side of waistband.

6. Sew stripe grosgrain ribbon 1/2" above hem, tacking jumbo red rickrack under ribbon edges so peaks show on each side of ribbon. Use a straight stitch on both sides of the ribbon.

7. Measure skirt width and divide by 12. Using this figure, evenly space and sew buttons 2" from hem—alternating red heart, white star, red heart, etc.

♥ *Note:* Measurements for rickrack and ribbon are correct for up to child's size 8. Increase yardage for larger sizes. Jeans jumper used was manufactured by Oshkosh B'Gosh. For best results, pre-wash jumper. Remove front bib pocket before starting to embellish jumper.

Shoes

(See Figure 3-1 and Color Pages)

Materials

Pair of red canvas slip-on shoes

1-1/2 yards 3/8" flat lace trim

1/2 yard 3/8" white/red/navy stripe grosgrain ribbon

Scraps of:

white piqué

navy mini-plaid fabric

Package Aleene's Hot Stitch Fusible Web Appliqué Pack

2 brass 1/4" jingle bells

2 red bow buttons or red satin bows (1/8" ribbon)

Acrylic paints in black and red

Bottle white Slick paint by Tulip Productions

0000 fine-line sable paintbrush

Pink Venus colored pencil

Disappearing ink marking pen

Aleene's Tacky Glue

Matching threads

Directions

1. Trim around shoe opening with white flat lace trim using one of these methods: gluing—use clothespins to hold lace in place while glue dries; or hand sewing—use strong double thread. Needle-nose pliers make it easier to pull needle through heavy canvas. Tie two bows with white/red/ navy stripe grosgrain ribbon and glue or sew bow to back of each shoe.

2. Following Aleene's Hot Stitch Fusible Web instructions, fuse to back of piqué scraps. Cut two white piqué cat faces (Figure 3-5). Stuff shoe firmly with towel or scrap fabric. Do not use plastic bags, as the heat from fusing can melt the plastic in shoe. Fuse cat face to shoe front using photo as a guide. *Hint:* Do not have iron filled with water when fusing appliqué to shoe front, as hot water can spill on you when you tilt the iron to securely fuse the

appliqué. Also take care not to have iron touch the rubber rim of shoe, as it can melt the rubber. Using white Slick paint, paint around edge of face. This method prevents fabric from fraying and also acts as an additional bond to shoe. Repeat for other shoe.

3. Draw in face with disappearing ink marking pen and paint as shown in Figure 3-5. Allow to dry completely. Lightly shade cheeks and ears with pink Venus colored pencil. Cut kerchief from navy mini-plaid fabric, turn under edges 1/4", and hem. Starting at your right, tack kerchief to appliqué and shoe, pleating and tacking to fit neckline, with tie end to extend to outside of shoe as shown in the photo. Tack or glue jingle bell to "knot" of kerchief. Tie small bow with 1/8" red satin ribbon (or use red bow button), and tack or glue above bell. Repeat for other shoe, reversing the direction of the kerchief.

4. To help shoes remain in good condition, spray with Scotchguard spray and repeat as needed.

♥ *Equipment suggested:* Needle-nose pliers, clothespins, and Scotchguard spray

♥ *Note:* Measurement for flat lace trim is accurate up to child's shoe size 11. Increase yardage for larger sizes.

♥ *Note:* When making shoes for children under 3, use double strand dental floss to secure buttons/bells in place for shoes.

Fig. 3-5

Kerchief for
Jumper Appliqué

Clever Kitty
Appliqué for
Jumper

Heart Appliqué
for Clever Kitty
Jumper

fold →

Kerchief for
Kitty face

Kitty face
for shoes,
raincoat and
umbrella

♥ Presto Pizzazz — It's Raining Cats and Dogs!

Here's a fast way to continue the theme of this season to include a purchased yellow rain slicker and hat, along with a child's brightly colored umbrella.

Fig. 3-6

Raining Cats and Dogs Slicker and Hat

Fig. 3-7

Materials

Yellow rain slicker with hat

Tulip Slick paints in white, pink, red, and black

2 yards 1/2" primary rainbow stripe grosgrain ribbon

1/2 yard 1/16" white satin ribbon

1/3 yard 1/8" red satin ribbon

Pencil

Matching threads

Equipment needed: Glass cleaner in spray spritzer and paper towels

Directions

1. Spray glass cleaner on paper towels and wipe off slicker to remove any residue or dirt. Wipe off hat in same manner.

2. Hand sew rainbow grosgrain ribbon around collar of slicker. Sew rainbow grosgrain ribbon across pocket flaps to trim.

3. Trace cat's face from Figure 3-5 onto paper and cut out for template. Repeat for dog (Figure 3-3), but cut three templates: one face, one right ear, and one left ear.

4. On left pocket, center template and trace around cat's face with a pencil. With white Slick paint, paint in cat's face. Allow to dry thoroughly.

5. While left pocket is drying, center face template for dog on right pocket and draw around with a pencil. Arrange ears on each side of face and trace around them with a pencil. With white Slick paint, paint in dog's face.

6. After paint has dried to the touch, paint in facial details of the cat, using black for the outlines, pink for cheeks and ears, and red for nose and tongue. Mix white and black on a paper plate and paint in gray ears for the dog. Allow to dry. Loop 1/16" white satin ribbon in 1-1/2" loops and hand tack at top midsection of dog's head. Cut 1/8" red satin ribbon into two 6" pieces, tie in bows, and tack under each animal's face.

7. For girls, add bows of rainbow grosgrain ribbon to top crease of each sleeve cuff. For boys, stitch rainbow grosgrain ribbon 1/2" from edge of each sleeve cuff, overlapping and tucking under ends.

8. For cap, paint one cat's face and one dog's face on front of hat brim, using above directions. Make four-loop bow of rainbow grosgrain ribbon and tack securely to top of cap.

Raining Cats and Dogs Umbrella

(See Figure 3-6)

Materials

Child's size primary color golf umbrella

Scraps of:

    white poplin

    navy mini-plaid fabric

    gray mini-print fabric

    red mini-plaid fabric

Package Aleene's Hot Stitch Fusible Web Appliqué Pack

4 brass 1/4" jingle bells

4 red bow buttons or red satin bows (1/8" ribbon)

2 yards 1/16" white satin ribbon

Tulip Slick paints in white, pink, red, and black

0000 fine-line sable paintbrush

Pink Venus colored pencil

Disappearing ink marking pen

Aleene's Tacky Glue

Matching threads

♥ *Note:* When embellishing umbrella for children under 3, use double strand of dental floss to secure buttons in place for animal faces instead of gluing.

Directions

1. This project shows a child's size golf umbrella with eight sections. You will appliqué two dog and two cat heads. If your umbrella has fewer or more sections, plan accordingly. Most umbrellas are made of polyester or nylon fabric which must be pressed at cooler temperatures. Test iron temperature on small snap piece before proceeding with fusing. Aleene's Hot Stitch Fusible Web will work at lower temperatures, but it takes a little more time for fusing. If your umbrella fabric cannot withstand temperatures for fusing, considering painting on cat and dog faces, following the instructions given for rain slicker.

2. Following Aleene's Hot Stitch Fusible Web instructions, back poplin and gray fabrics. Cut two white poplin dog heads and four ears from gray mini-print (two in reverse), using the shapes in Figure 3-3. Fuse head and ears to umbrella, at first and fifth umbrella segments, 2-1/2" above bottom, following the pattern. *Hint:* Do not have iron filled with water when fusing appliqué to umbrella, as hot water can spill on you when you tilt the iron to securely fuse the appliqué. Using white Slick paint, paint around edge of face and ears. This method prevents fabric from fraying and also acts as an additional bond to umbrella. Wrap 1/16" white satin ribbon around two fingers six times, slip off, and tie in center. Fold loops in V at tie point and tack to top of dog's head for fluffy hair. Repeat for other appliqué.

3. Draw in dog face with disappearing ink marking pen and paint as shown in Figure 3-3. Use black for features and red for tongue; lightly shade cheeks with pink Venus colored pencil. Allow to dry completely. Cut kerchief from red mini-plaid fabric, turn under edges 1/4", and hem. Starting at your right, tack kerchief to appliqué and umbrella, pleating and tacking to fit neck, with tie end to extend to left as shown in the photo. Tack or glue small 1/4" bow button or ribbon bow to "knot" of kerchief with jingle bell on top. Repeat for other dog appliqué.

4. Cut two white poplin cat faces (Figure 3-5). Fuse cat face to third and seventh umbrella segments 2-1/2" above bottom. Using white Slick paint, paint around edge of face. Repeat for other cat appliqué.

5. Draw in face with disappearing ink marking pen and paint as shown in Figure 3-5. Use black to outline and for eyes; use pink for nose, and red for mouth. Lightly shade cheeks and inner ears with pink Venus colored pencil. Allow to dry completely. Cut kerchief from navy mini-plaid fabric, turn under edges 1/4", and hem. Starting at your right, tack kerchief to appliqué and umbrella, pleating and tacking to fit neckline, with tie end to extend to left as shown in the photo. Tie small bow with 1/8" red satin ribbon (or use red bow button), and tack or glue to "knot" of kerchief with jingle bell on top. Repeat for other cat appliqué.

4. Swinging into Summer

Don't you love watching the glee on a toddler's face as he or she first discovers the joys of summer? Children revel in the endless hours at the park, eyes glowing at the sights of a garden in bloom, fingers snatching at a butterfly floating on the wind, faces smiling as they splash in the wading pool. Their clothing can reflect the same bright spirit that the days ahead hold.

The one question I am asked more than any other is, "Where do you get your ideas?" Using the bright pastels of summer, let me show you how the designs for this chapter evolved. Each design is coordinated with a matching pair of sneakers. You'll find you can use these same design techniques to create a wardrobe of wonder and fun. With this design method and your own fabric and notions collection, you can stitch delightful designs. Both boys' and girls' wardrobes can be put together with the same techniques. Don't be afraid to experiment.

This chapter includes directions on a patchwork jumper and matching shoes,

Fig. 4-1

boy's outfit featuring overalls and shoes, girl's sundress with painted shoes, and a quick sailor teddy shirt with shorts.

♥ *Patchwork Pizzazz*
Jumper
Painted Shoes

♥ *Plane Pizzazz*
Appliquéd Overalls
Painted Shoes

♥ *Buttons 'n Ribbons 'n Bows, Oh My!*
Sundress
Painted Shoes

♥ *Presto Pizzazz for Summer*
Sailor Teddy T-shirt
Sailor Shorts

♥ *Patchwork Pizzazz*

Fig. 4-2

Jumper/Sundress

(See Color Pages)

♥ *Note:* When making this outfit for a toddler under 3, attach shoulder buttons with dental floss and delete worm button on flower.

While organizing my sewing closet (for the umpteenth time), I found several prints from previous projects that complemented each other beautifully. There wasn't enough yardage per piece to complete a garment; but by combining the fabrics with stylish touches, I found the design idea came to life.

The white and blue chintz solids were perfect mates for a checkerboard pieced strip, the pink heart print brought mental pictures of hearts, flowers, and a slice of watermelon, and the pretty checks and gridwork fabrics could tie the whole design together. The ideas fell into place as I worked. By taking each segment of the pieced jumper/sundress separately, you'll be pleasantly surprised at how easily and quickly this garment goes together.

Materials

Purchased pattern for simple A-line, lined jumper/sundress

5/8 yard white with light blue square gridwork cotton

5/8 yard blue/pink/white floral mini-print cotton

1/8 yard light blue solid chintz

1/8 yard white solid chintz

1/4 yard white/light blue crayon check print cotton

Scraps of:

    pink heart print fabric

    green mini-dot print cotton

    green mini-stripe cotton

    white jumbo rickrack

    lightweight iron-on interfacing

Package Aleene's Hot Stitch Fusible Web Appliqué Pack

Green squiggly worm button

2 white 1" bunny buttons with pink flowers

White tissue paper and #2 pencil

Matching threads

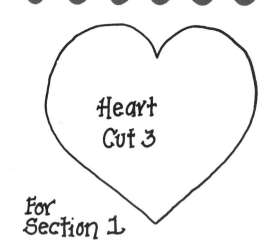

Heart
Cut 3

For
Section 1

Fig. 4-3

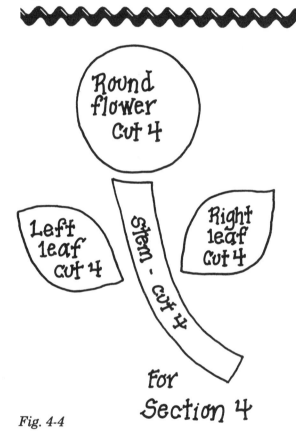

Round
flower
cut 4

Left
leaf
cut 4

stem - cut 4

Right
leaf
cut 4

For
Section 4

Fig. 4-4

Directions

1. Prewash all fabrics; lightly press as needed. Trace front dress piece, complete with seam allowances. This design divides the dress front into four sections, which you'll mark on your first tissue pattern. Draw a line across upper area of dress from bottom of armhole on left side to bottom of armhole on right side. Measure and mark a line 2" below first drawn line—this section is for the checkerboard strip. Next, go to curved hemline of dress and measure 4-1/2" from hem. Mark measurement every 1-1/2" and connect curved line. This tissue pattern will be your master for the pieced dress. Label Sections 1, 2, 3, and 4, starting at top of dress.

2. On another sheet of tissue paper, trace Section 1. Add 1/4" seam allowance to bottom of piece. Trace Section 3 and add 1/4" seam allowance to top and bottom of piece. Trace Section 4 and add 1/4" seam allowance to top of curved piece.

3. Cut out one front piece and one back piece from white gridwork cotton (for dress lining) and one Section 3 from the same fabric. From blue/pink/white mini-floral print cut one right side back piece and one Section 1. For checkerboard strip, cut one strip each 1-1/2" x 20" of light blue and of white chintz. Cut one curved piece for Section 4 from white/light blue crayon check print.

4. Back pink heart print, green mini-stripe, and green mini-dot fabrics with lightweight iron-on interfacing. Trace three hearts, one main watermelon slice, and four round flowers (Figures 4-3 through 4-5) on paper backing of Aleene's Hot Stitch Fusible Web. Fuse to the wrong side of the pink heart print, centering the round flowers on a heart, and cut out appliqués. In same manner, trace, fuse, and cut one watermelon rind from green mini-stripe, as well as four flower stems and eight leaves from green mini-dot.

5. Peel paper backing from three heart appliqués, space evenly across Section 1, and fuse in place. Cut piece of lightweight iron-on interfacing slightly larger than appliqué area and fuse to wrong side of

Fig. 4-5

Patchwork Pizzazz
Summer Jumper

Watermelon Slice
for Section 3

Watermelon
Rind

Section 1 underneath appliqués. Appliqué hearts with medium-width satin stitch and matching threads. Press.

6. The checkerboard pieced strip for Section 2 uses blue and white chintz strips. With right sides together, sew strips together lengthwise using 1/4" seam allowance. Press seam open. Cut sewn strip into 1-1/2" wide segments. Sew segments together, alternating colors on top for checkerboard design, using 1/4" seam allowance. Press.

7. Peel off paper backing for watermelon slice and rind, position, and fuse to center of Section 3 gridwork print fabric. Cut a piece of lightweight iron-on interfacing slightly larger than appliqué area and fuse to wrong side of piece underneath appliqué area. Sew appliqué using medium-width satin stitch and matching threads. Press.

8. Section 4 has four round flowers evenly spaced across the piece. Peel off paper backing from flowers, stems, and leaves, position, and fuse to bottom curved crayon check print piece. Cut and fuse a piece of lightweight iron-on interfacing slightly larger than the appliqué area to the wrong side of the piece underneath the appliqués. Appliqué flowers, stems, and leaves with matching threads and medium-width satin stitch. Baste white jumbo rickrack to top edge of curved piece with 1/8" seam allowance. Tack squiggly worm button to leaf of second flower from your right.

9. With 1/4" seam allowance, sew sections together with right sides together. Press seams open. Following purchased pattern instructions, complete garment. Use bunny buttons at shoulder. Press.

Sneakers

(See Figure 4-2 and Color Pages)

Materials

Pair of white canvas sneakers

2 yards each:

    1/16" blue satin ribbon

    1/8" green satin ribbon

    1/4" pink satin ribbon

Tulip Slick paints in pink, white, green, black, and light blue

0000 fine line sable paintbrush

Disappearing ink marking pen

Paper plate

Scotchguard spray

Directions

1. Unlace shoes and firmly stuff with paper or plastic grocery bags. With disappearing ink marking pen, draw in hearts, round flowers with stems, watermelon slices, and ladybugs in a miscellaneous pattern (see Figure 4-6). If you're not pleased with your first results, wipe shoes with dampened towel to erase, dry thoroughly, and start again.

2. Squirt paints onto paper plate for palette. Paint shoes using dress colors and design for examples. Be careful not to have different wet colors touching each other as the colors will run together. Allow to dry and add finishing touches of dots, swirls, and details for ladybug.

3. Spray shoes liberally with Scotchguard spray. Cut ribbons into 1-yard pieces. Lace shoe treating all three ribbons as one. Repeat for other shoe.

Fig. 4-6

Painting guideline for patchwork pizzazz sneakers

♥ *Plane Pizzazz*

When I saw the fabric used for these overalls, I was airborne with delight. Bright, yet simple, this print could be used for several mix-and-match outfits. Use leftover scraps backed with lightweight iron-on interfacing as simple appliqué designs to coordinate with other garments. The cutouts can be sewn on T-shirt fronts and sleeves, or can add spice to pockets trimmed with coordinating rickrack or piping. You can use the same idea with any shape from a patterned fabric—blow up the shape and appliqué it as a center of interest.

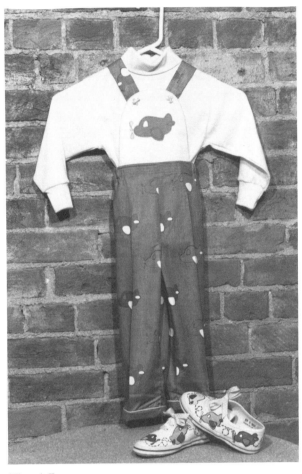

Fig. 4-7

Overalls

(See Figure 4-7)

♥ *Note:* For young toddlers who are not potty trained, leave crotch seam open, sewing snap tape to each side of underleg, for easy diaper changes.

Materials

Purchased overalls pattern with curved bib and leg cuffs

3/4 yard light blue with pastel airplane print fabric

1/4 yard white sailcloth or poplin

1/8 yard bright green chintz

Scraps of:
  light blue chintz
  pink chintz
  yellow chintz
  lightweight iron-on interfacing
  fusible webbing

Package of yellow piping

2 yellow airplane buttons

1/2 yard 3/4" white elastic

Matching threads

Directions

1. Prewash all fabrics; lightly press as needed. Cut front pants, back pants, and straps from airplane print; two cuffs from green chintz, and two bibs of white sailcloth.

2. Back chintz scraps with lightweight iron-on interfacing and cut out appliqués as follows (see Figure 4-8):

> main plane, light blue chintz
> tail and wing, pink chintz
> propeller, yellow chintz

3. Position and fuse plane appliqué to center of bib by tucking small pieces of fusible webbing under appliqués. Cut a piece of lightweight iron-on interfacing slightly larger than appliqué area and fuse to wrong side of bib underneath appliqués. With matching threads, stitch around main plane with medium-width satin stitch. Wing, tail, and propeller are appliquéd with matching threads and narrow-width satin stitches. Press.

4. Baste yellow piping around sides and top of bib with 1/4" seam allowance. Pin bib and lining with right sides together and stitch around sides and top, following the pattern seam allowance. Turn right side out and press.

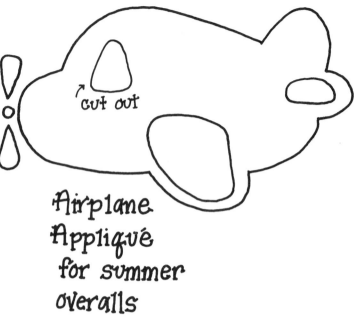

Airplane
Appliqué
for summer
overalls

Fig. 4-8

5. Following your purchased pattern instructions, stitch overalls and straps, leaving crotch seam open. Trim bottom of pant legs with yellow piping, using 1/4" seam allowance. Sew contrasting green chintz cuffs to pant legs. Sew crotch seam and hem pant legs per pattern.

Knee Patches

Does your little tot spend as much time scooting around on hands and knees as walking? Padded knee patches of same or contrasting fabric can prolong the life of your garment.

Materials

Scraps from overalls or contrasting
    Trigger or sailcloth

1/8 yard bonded polyfil batting

1/8 yard fusible webbing

Yellow piping

Matching threads

Directions

1. Fuse batting to wrong side of plane (or contrasting) fabric. Cut two oval patches. Trim edges of ovals with yellow piping using 1/4" seam allowance. Turn and fold piping to outside edge and topstitch with 1/8" seam allowance.

2. Pin and baste to knee areas of overalls. Sew securely to knees by stitching-in-the-ditch between piping and patch. Machine or hand quilt around airplanes in channel design.

Sneakers

(See Figure 4-7)

Materials

Pair of white or light blue sneakers

1-1/2 yards 3/8" yellow with white dot grosgrain ribbon

Tulip Slick paints in hot pink, bright yellow, bright green, light blue, and purple

Scotchguard spray

Disappearing ink marking pen

Directions

1. Wipe sneakers with damp towel to remove any dirt or residue. Remove laces and stuff shoes firmly with paper or plastic bags.

2. Trace around airplane pattern (see Figure 4-9) and cut out for template; repeat for tail and wing. With disappearing ink marking pen, trace around plane template on shoe several times as shown in Figure 4-7. Draw in dotted lines for loop-de-loop twirls and twists.

3. Shake paint bottles so paint is well mixed. Color in planes with assorted colors. Allow paint to dry as instructed by the manufacturer. Paint in wing, tail, and propeller detail in contrasting colors. Dotted lines are painted with light blue paint. Allow to dry overnight.

4. Spray shoes liberally with Scotchguard spray. Cut yellow grosgrain ribbons into two 3/4-yard pieces and lace shoes.

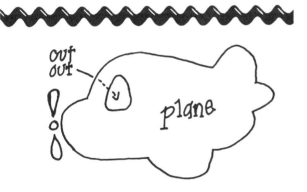

Airplane pattern for Sneakers

Fig. 4-9

♥ *Hint:* Dip ribbon lace ends in clear nail polish and allow to dry to keep ribbon lace ends from fraying.

♥ Buttons 'n Ribbons 'n Bows, Oh My!

Your ribbon and button box can be the basis of an outfit. Collect an assortment of odds and ends that are compatible. Different sizes, shapes, and colors of buttons will add visual impact. Ribbons can be different widths and styles that complement each other.

Fig. 4-10

Buttons 'n Bows Sundress

(See Figure 4-10)

Materials

Purchased pattern for jumper with front/ back yokes and gathered skirt

1/4 yard white Trigger or sailcloth

3/4 yard light blue/white seersucker or oxford stripe

Package pink piping

White 9" zipper

Assortment of 25–30 buttons

1 yard 1/16" white satin ribbon

1-1/2 yards 3/8" hot pink dot grosgrain ribbon

1-1/2 yards 3/8" pastel stripe grosgrain ribbon

White tissue paper and #2 pencil

Matching threads

Directions

1. Prewash all fabrics and piping; lightly press as needed. Trace skirt front and skirt back pieces on tissue paper, including seam allowances. Using drawn tissue patterns, measure from bottom of front skirt 1-1/4" from hemline edge and mark at 1" intervals. Connect lines. Measure border 2-1/2" above first line and mark. Repeat in same manner for back skirt piece. These are your master patterns. Label sections for skirt front Sections 1, 2, and 3, and back Sections 1, 2, and 3.

2. One by one, trace both front and back sections to another tissue sheet, adding seam allowances, and label pieces. For both front and back skirt Sections 1, add 1/4" seam allowance to bottom of piece. Add 1/4" seam allowance to both top and bottom of front and back Sections 2. To the bottom Sections 3, add a 1/4" seam allowance to the top only.

3. Cut front bodice and back bodice pieces, front skirt Section 2, and back skirt Section 2, from white Trigger. Using light blue/ white stripe, cut front skirt Sections 1 and 3, back skirt Sections 1 and 3, two armhole bindings, and neckline binding.

4. Sew the side seam separately for Sections 1, 2, and 3. Trim top and bottom edges

of Section 2 with pink piping using 1/8"
seam allowance. Sew Sections 1, 2, and 3
together with 1/4" seam allowances and
right sides together. Press.

5. Assemble dress, following the purchased pattern instructions. On a table,
arrange buttons in clusters of three to five
buttons. Cut 3/8" ribbons into 18" and 36"
pieces. Make double loop bows using 18"
pieces with long streamers. Tack hot pink
grosgrain bow to right side of skirt Section
2. Twist and curl streamers. Tack streamers in place with buttons as shown in Figure
4-10. In the same manner tack and trim
pastel stripe bow to back of skirt Section 2.
Add button clusters going around entire
Section 2, saving two clusters for bodice.

6. Tie four-loop bows with 36" pieces and
tack to each other through bow centers.
Make six-loop bow of 1/16" white satin
ribbon and tack to center of other bows.
Securely sew multi-loop bow to left side of
bodice at seamline. Add button clusters to
embellish bodice. Lightly press.

♥ *Note:* If making this outfit for a
young toddler, sew on buttons with
dental floss for most secure attachment. If you feel your fabric might
tear if buttons are pulled, fuse some
stiff iron-on interfacing to wrong side
of fabric for better results.

Buttons 'n Bows Sneakers

(See Figure 4-10)

Materials

Pair of children's light blue/white striped
    sneakers

Tulip Slick paints in fluorescent pink,
    fluorescent green, light blue, royal blue,
    yellow, lavender, black, and white

0000 fine-line sable paintbrush

Paper towels and paper plate

1-1/4 yards 3/8" white satin novelty print
    ribbon

Disappearing ink marking pen

Scotchguard spray

Directions

1. Remove shoelaces and stuff shoes
firmly with plastic grocery bags or paper.
Using Figures 4-10 and 4-11 as guides, use
the disappearing ink marking pen to draw
design on shoes. Bows are drawn with two
rounded triangles with an oval in the center
for the loop of the knot. Streamers are
wavy lines or ovals. Buttons can be circles,
squares, or ovals—with hearts and stars

added for novelty buttons. Use your own
button box for inspiration. If you are un-
happy with your first design, dampen the
drawn area to erase, dry thoroughly, and
begin again.

2. Using a paper plate as your palette,
squirt little blobs of paint in each color on
the plate. Using the fine-line paintbrush,
paint in main shape of bows with fluorescent pink with random buttons in colors you
prefer. **Make sure your wet painted
areas do not overlap, as paints will run
together.** Canvas shoes absorb the
paints—don't worry if your paints seem dull
or hardly visible. You can add three to four
coats of paint for a durable, bright finish.
This is a great pick-up project, needing only
a few minutes to add extra coats of paint.

3. After solid buttons and bows are painted
with several coats and dried, you can begin
outlining the bows and adding details.
Using the fine-line paintbrush and black
paint, outline the bow, adding detail as
shown in the illustration. Using the wooden
end of the paintbrush, dip into the white
paint and add white polka dots to the
painted ribbons. Add little "comma" shapes
at the rounded corners of the ribbon bows
for highlight.

4. Outline buttons in contrasting colors.
You can mix colors on your paper-plate

Fig. 4-11

Painting guideline for Buttons 'n Bows sneakers

palette for added variety. Add inner details to buttons with stripes or dots, and highlight with "comma" shape in white for shine.

5. Add extra coats of paint to outline as needed. Allow to dry thoroughly—overnight is best. Spray liberally with Scotchguard

spray, wait an hour, and repeat with a second coat of Scotchguarding for extra protection.

6. Cut novelty ribbon in half and use for shoelaces.

♥ *Presto Pizzazz for Summer*

This sailor ensemble is perfect for your little mate, boy or girl. Each piece can be sewn in an hour. That's what I call instant pizzazz!

Fig. 4-12

Sailor Teddy T-Shirt

(See Figure 4-12)

Materials

Red purchased T-shirt
Scraps of:
tan velour
red/white mini-stripe fabric
royal blue sailcloth
brown mini-dot fabric
red mini-dot fabric
white mini-rickrack
3/8" red dot grosgrain ribbon
lightweight iron-on interfacing
fusible webbing
brown embroidery floss
8 royal blue 1/2" star buttons
2 white anchor buttons
8 white 1/4" star buttons
2 black 6-mm beads
Pink Venus colored pencil
Matching threads

Directions

1. Back fabric scraps with lightweight iron-on interfacing and cut out appliqué pieces as follows (Figure 4-13):

teddy face, tan velour
sailor collar, blue sailcloth
sailor dickey, red/white mini-stripe
two ears (one in reverse), red mini-dot
one nose, brown mini-dot

2. Position teddy face, collar, and dickey on shirt front. Cut pieces of fusible webbing and tuck under appliqué pieces. Fuse appliqués to shirt. Cut white mini-rickrack to trim collar as in Figure 4-12 and stitch in place. Cut a piece of lightweight iron-on interfacing slightly larger than appliqué area and fuse to wrong side of shirt underneath appliqué area. With matching threads, appliqué sailor teddy with medium-width satin stitch. Position, fuse, and appliqué ears and nose to face with narrow-width satin stitch. Stitch black beads for eyes very securely (use dental floss for children under 3 years of age). Embroider mouth with two strands brown embroidery floss in straight stitch. Color in cheeks with pink Venus colored pencil. With 5" length of red dot grosgrain ribbon, tie knot in center of ribbon and tack to pointed end of dickey. Cut ribbon ends in V shape. Lightly press.

3. Sew anchor buttons to sleeves at cuff crease. Alternate white and blue star buttons evenly spaced around sleeve cuffs and neckline as seen in Figure 4-12. Do not sew any buttons to sleeve cuff underarm seam—they rub and can be uncomfortable for your toddler.

Sailor Shorts

(See Figure 4-12)

Materials

Purchased pattern for simple shorts
    with cuff

1/2 yard royal blue sailcloth

1/8 yard red mini-dot cotton

4 red 1" star appliqués

Red 1" anchor appliqué

1/2 yard 3/4" white elastic

Matching threads

Directions

1.   Prewash fabrics; lightly press as necessary. Cut front and back for shorts from
royal blue sailcloth. Cut two cuffs from red
mini-dot fabric.

2.   Sew shorts with cuffs following your
pattern instructions. Topstitch front waistband.

3.   Fuse four evenly spaced red star appliqués across front of waistband. Fuse red
anchor appliqué to middle of left short leg
(Figure 4-12).

♥   *Note:* If appliqués are not heat set,
use Aleene's Hot Stitch Fusible Web
to add fusible backing to appliqués,
using package directions to heat set.

Fig. 4-13

Sailor Teddy
T-shirt
appliqué for
summer

Presto
Pizzazz

dickey

rickrack

sailor
collar

5. *Anchored to Autumn*

When it's time to get your youngsters ready for a new fall season, every moment counts. Catching the last lightning bug of the season, assembling a new array of beginner's school supplies, and that wonderful season-ending trek to the swimming pool—all these things capture our moments. For those busy back-to-school days, here are some projects that use ready-made items—just waiting for your own brand of personal style. Yet these nautical-theme separates are quick and easy-to-do, adding that dash of class we all love to see our children wear.

Please keep in mind that the projects shown here are merely one suggestion of what you can do with these appliqué designs. The nautical overalls appliqué would be equally cute on the back of a white terrycloth robe; the first mate appliqué could jazz up a knit nightshirt; and the lighthouse scene would be delightful on a sweatsuit or rugby shirt.

Get to work quickly by starting with purchased garments and then embellishing them. Directions in this chapter cover a sweatshirt, sweater, overalls, sailor cap with matching knee socks, and a trio of sweaters.

Fig. 5-1

♥ *Anchors Aweigh*
Sweatshirt
Sweater
Overalls

♥ *Nautical Accessories*
Sailor Cap
Knee Socks

♥ *Sweater Savvy*
Tartan Trim
Duck Appliqué
Crested View

♥ Anchors Aweigh

Fig. 5-2

First Mate Sweatshirt

(See Figure 5-2 and Color Pages)

Materials

White acrylic sweatshirt
2-1/4 yards 1" red/white mini-check ribbon
1-1/8 yards royal blue medium-size rickrack
6 red 1/2" ship's wheel buttons
8 red 5-mm round wooden beads
1 yard 1/8" yellow satin ribbon
Blue sailboat button
Red 1-1/2" Dolly duck button
Scraps of:
    white solid poplin
    royal blue solid poplin
    red mini-dot fabric
    red mini-stripe fabric
    unbleached muslin
    lightweight iron-on interfacing
    royal blue and red embroidery floss
Package Aleene's Hot Stitch Fusible Web
    Appliqué Pack
Pink Venus colored pencil
Disappearing ink marking pen
Matching threads

Directions

1. Cut red/white mini-check ribbon into one 41" piece for neckline and two 20" pieces for wrist cuffs. Lightly gather 41" ribbon piece along ribbon edge and sew to neckline with a narrow zigzag just below ribbing. Be sure to stretch knit as you attach gathered ribbon trim. Stitch 20-1/2" piece of royal blue rickrack along top edge of ribbon with a narrow zigzag, stretching as you stitch. *Note:* If you don't stretch the neckline as you stitch, you won't be able to fit the sweatshirt over the child's head. Sew four red ship's wheel buttons along trim line, using raglan sleeve seams for placement guide.

2. Lightly gather 20" ribbon pieces for wrist cuffs and stitch to sweatshirt at cuff line where sleeve attaches to ribbing cuff. If you have a free-arm sewing machine, just slip the cuff on the free arm and stitch with a narrow zigzag. Trim cuff on top of ribbon with 10" piece royal blue rickrack using a narrow zigzag. Repeat for other arm. Stitch red ship's wheel button to each arm at trimming edge using sleeve center crease line as a guide.

3. Back fabric scraps with Aleene's Hot Stitch Fusible Web and cut out appliqués as follows (Figure 5-3):

    face and two hands, unbleached muslin
    cap and sailor collar, white solid poplin
    two arms (one in reverse), red mini-
      dot fabric
    dickey and two legs, red mini-stripe
      fabric
    main dress and two shoes, royal blue
      solid poplin

Position and fuse appliqué to front of sweatshirt, **omitting cap.**

4. Cut a piece of lightweight iron-on interfacing slightly larger than entire appliqué scene and fuse to **wrong** side of sweatshirt **underneath** appliqué scene. Using matching threads and medium-width satin stitch, appliqué design. With disappearing ink marking pen, draw in eyes and smile as shown in Figure 5-3. Embroider eyes with satin stitch using two strands of royal blue embroidery floss. For smile, embroider with two strands of red embroidery floss using stem stitch. Lightly shade cheeks with pink Venus colored pencil.

5. For hair, start at top left side of face and tack four loops of yellow satin ribbon 1" long. Continue making small 3/8" loops for bangs, tacking ribbon at top of head as you go across face piece. At right side of face, make four more 1" loops and tack in place. Fuse cap in place at an angle as shown in Figure 5-3. Cap should just cover tacked ends of ribbon hair. Draw topstitching detail for cap with disappearing ink marking pen and appliqué outline with red thread and medium-width satin stitch. Add topstitching detail using red thread and narrow-width satin stitch.

6. Tie 2-1/2" piece of yellow ribbon with knot in center and tack at sailor collar's bottom point. Sew six red wooden beads in place for buttons on main dress (see Figure 5-3). Tie two small bows of yellow ribbon and tack to outside top corners of shoes with red wooden beads for trim. Lightly press. *Note:* If you're making this sweatshirt for a child under 3 years of age, omit wooden beads and embroider French knots with three strands of embroidery floss instead.

7. Add small sailboat button sewn to right hand. Dolly duck button is tacked to your bottom right of appliqué scene. Pull and trim excess interfacing from wrong side of sweatshirt.

♥ *Laundering Tip:* Pretreat all stains as soon as possible. Turn sweatshirt inside out and launder on gentle cycle. Dry flat on drying rack or tumble dry on permanent press setting. Lightly steam press using press cloth as necessary.

Note: Shoes are cut out so red mini-stripe shows.

• red wooden beads
OR french knots

First Mate Sweatshirt Appliqué - Autumn
For girls, trim along top of head with yellow satin ribbon per written instructions for hair.
For boys, trim along top of head with 3/8" loops of yellow satin ribbon for hair.

Fig. 5-3

Lighthouse Scene Sweater

(See Color Pages)

Fig. 5-4

Materials

Acrylic or cotton royal blue cableknit
  sweater
1-1/4 yard 10-mm white cotton cable cording
3 red 1" star appliqués
Red 1-1/2" star appliqué
White 1/4" star button
Scraps of:
  white piqué
  red mini-stripe fabric
  yellow solid poplin
  red mini-dot fabric
  green mini-stripe fabric
  light blue mini-check gingham
  royal blue dot fabric
  lightweight iron-on interfacing
Package Aleene's Hot Stitch Fusible Web
  Appliqué Pack
Disappearing ink marking pen
Matching threads

Directions

1. With disappearing ink marking pen, dot
cording at 9", 18", and 27" measurements.
Tie a knot at each dot, making sure your
knots are all tied going the same direction.
Using center back of sweater for first measurement, divide neckline into three equal
parts and pin-mark. Tack cording knots at
each pin mark. Lightly swag spaces between knots and tack in center of swag to
bottom of neckline ribbing with 1" red star
appliqués. For extra strength, machine tack
through center of knots. Slipstitch cording
ends together. *Note:* You'll have a swag
look here. It's very important to have slack
so you can fit sweater over child's head.

2. Back fabric scraps with Aleene's Hot
Stitch Fusible Web and cut out appliqués as
follows (Figure 5-5):

  two seagulls, white piqué
  lighthouse top and main tower, red
    mini-stripe fabric **cut on diagonal**
  left sail, green mini-stripe fabric **cut on
    diagonal**
  right sail, red mini-dot fabric
  lighthouse light and sailboat bottom,
    yellow solid poplin
  top wave, light blue mini-check gingham
  bottom wave, royal blue dot fabric

3. Using Figures 5-4 and 5-5 as guides,
position and fuse appliqués to sweater front.
Cut a piece of lightweight iron-on interfacing slightly larger than appliqué scene and
fuse to wrong side of sweater underneath
appliqué scene.

4. Appliqué pieces using matching threads
and medium-width satin stitch. Tack white
star button to red mini-dot sail. Pull and
trim excess interfacing from wrong side of
sweater. Sew 1-1/2" star appliqué to sleeve.
Lightly steam press.

♥ *Laundering Tip:* Pretreat all stains as
  soon as possible. Turn sweater inside
  out and launder on gentle cycle. Dry flat
  on drying rack or tumble dry (while still
  inside out) on permanent press setting.
  Turn right side out and steam press
  using press cloth as necessary.

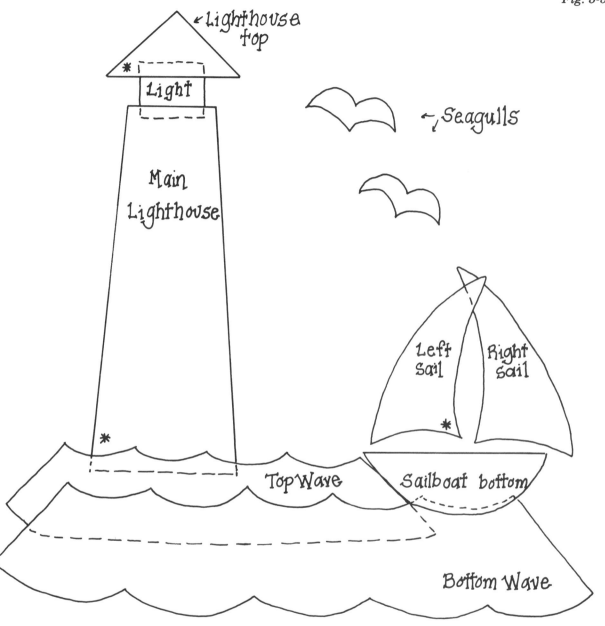

Fig. 5-5

Lighthouse Sweater Appliqué – Autumn

* Mini-stripe pieces: cut on diagonal.

Nautical Overalls

(See Color Pages)

Fig. 5-6

♥ **Note:** If making this outfit for a young toddler, sew on buttons with dental floss for most secure attachment. If you feel your fabric might tear if buttons are pulled, fuse some stiff iron-on interfacing under wrong side of fabric before sewing on buttons for best results.

Materials

Pair red bib overalls
1/4 yard royal blue dot fabric
Scraps of:
 light blue mini-check gingham
 white piqué
 green mini-stripe fabric
 red mini-dot fabric
 yellow solid poplin
2/3 yard kelly green piping
1/2 yard red medium-width rickrack
Package Aleene's Hot Stitch Fusible Web Appliqué Pack
10 white 1/4" star buttons
Navy blue 1/4" star button
Purchased nautical appliqué for back pocket
1 yard 5/8" red/green stripe print ribbon
Matching threads

Directions

1. Back 7" square of royal blue dot fabric and fabric scraps with Aleene's Hot Stitch Fusible Web and cut out appliqués as follows (see Figure 5-7):

 outer circle, royal blue dot fabric
 inner circle, light blue mini-check gingham
 seagull, white piqué
 left sail, green mini-stripe fabric **cut on diagonal**
 right sail, red mini-dot fabric
 sailboat bottom, yellow solid poplin

2. Baste green piping to edge of royal blue dot circle, overlapping and tucking in ends. Baste red medium-width rickrack to edge of light blue mini-check gingham circle so peaks just show. **Note:** If your overalls have a pocket or decorative label on the bib, remove them now and steam press bib. You need to appliqué on a flat surface.

3. Position and fuse royal blue outer circle to center of bib. It's OK if circle extends to waistband, depending on the size and style of overalls you're trimming. Appliqué outer circle along edge of fabric and inside the piping. (The piping is not covered by satin stitches.)

Fig. 5-7

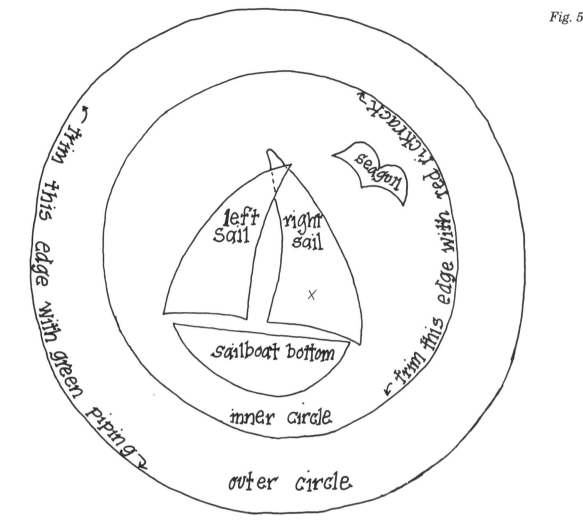

Nautical Overalls Appliqué
for Autumn

4. Position and fuse inner light blue gingham circle as shown in Figure 5-7. Appliqué along fabric edge, not on the rickrack. Position and fuse sailboat scene appliqué pieces to center of inner circle. Appliqué with medium-width satin stitch and matching threads. Press lightly. Sew navy blue star button to red mini-dot sail.

5. Trim waistband and pockets with white star buttons using Figure 5-6 as a guide. Sew stripe ribbon with a staight stitch along middle of overall straps. Tack nautical appliqué to back pocket.

♥ Nautical Accessories

Fig. 5-8

When you see how quick and easy it is to stitch up these darling matching nautical accessories, you'll be thrilled with the results.

Beribboned Sailor Cap

Materials

Red sailor's cap (white or navy cap works nicely, too)

2-1/2 yards 3/4" red/white/blue striped grosgrain ribbon (**Note:** Any wider width does not work as well as the slope of the cap requires easing of ribbon along bottom edge.)

1 yard 3/8" red/blue grosgrain stripe ribbon

1 yard 1/8" blue mini-dot satin ribbon

Red helm button

Aleene's Tacky All-Purpose glue

Matching threads

Directions

1. Center ribbon around turned-up brim of cap and hand stitch ribbon to cap along upper and lower edges of ribbon, overlapping and tucking under ends.

2. Make a four-loop bow with red/white/blue striped grosgrain, cutting ends at angles. Make additional four-loop bow of red/blue stripe ribbon and six-loop bow of blue mini-dot ribbon. Stack bows, matching up centers as in Figure 5-8 and tack together.

3. Glue bow to cap at ribbon overlap and allow to dry completely. Glue red helm button to center of bow.

Beribboned Nautical Knee Socks

Materials

Pair white acrylic knee socks

1 yard 1-1/4" red/white/blue gingham taffeta ribbon

1-1/2 yards 3/8" royal blue picot satin ribbon

1 yard 1/8" red mini-dot grosgrain ribbon

2 red helm buttons

2 baby-size safety pins

Matching threads

Directions

1. Cut all ribbons in half. Starting with gingham taffeta ribbon, make two two-loop bows. Make two four-loop blue picot bows and two four-loop red mini-dot grosgrain bows.

2. Stack bows, matching up centers with gingham taffeta bow on bottom, blue picot bow in middle, and red mini-dot grosgrain bow on top. Tack bows together through bow centers. Tack red helm button to center of bow. Repeat for other bow.

3. Pin bow (from inside sock) to top of outer side of each sock.

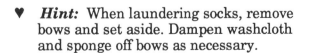

♥ *Hint:* When laundering socks, remove bows and set aside. Dampen washcloth and sponge off bows as necessary.

♥ *Presto Pizzazz — Sweater Savvy*

Starting with a basic cardigan of your choice, you'll love the way simple scraps, trims, and a trip to your button box will turn basics into beauties.

Fig. 5-9

Tartan Trimmed Sweater

(See Figure 5-9)

Materials

White cardigan
3/4 yard 1" red plaid taffeta ribbon
1/2 yard 3/8" green picot ribbon
5 red tartan plaid 1/2" buttons
Matching threads

Directions

1. Remove original buttons and replace with red tartan plaid buttons. Cut five 3" pieces green picot ribbon. Fold 3" pieces in half and crease. Twist each end, bring to center crease, fold in slight V, and tack. Sew folded V ribbon just under each buttonhole for leaves. Repeat for each buttonhole.

2. Tuck under each end of red plaid taffeta ribbon piece 1/4". Gather long edge of ribbon to fit bottom edge of neckline sweater ribbing. Adjust gathers evenly, and pin to bottom of sweater neckline ribbing. Sew by hand along gathered ribbon edge to sweater.

Just Ducky Sweater

(See Figure 5-9)

Materials

Navy blue cardigan sweater
3/4 yard 3/4" white gathered eyelet lace
5 red with white flowers 1/2" heart buttons
1/2 yard 3/8" red plaid ribbon
Scraps of:
   white piqué
   yellow poplin
   fusible webbing
   lightweight iron-on interfacing
   tear-away interfacing
   navy blue embroidery floss
Press cloth
Disappearing ink marking pen
Matching threads

Directions

1.   Remove original buttons from sweater and replace with red heart buttons.

2.   Hand stitch eyelet lace to right side front of sweater and each cuff, stretching cuffs slightly as you stitch.

3.   Back fabric scraps with lightweight iron-on interfacing. Cut one duck from white piqué. Cut duckbill and feet from yellow poplin (see Figure 5-10). Draw in eye, wing, and foot topstitching with disappearing ink marking pen. Position and fuse duck appliqué to upper left side of sweater front, using press cloth. Cut piece of tear-away interfacing slightly larger than appliqué area and pin to wrong side of sweater front underneath appliqué. Using yellow thread, appliqué duck, bill, and feet with medium-width satin stitch. Add topstitching details. Remove tear-away interfacing. Embroider eye with two strands navy blue embroidery floss and satin stitch. Press.

4.   Cut plaid ribbon into three 6" pieces. Tie three bows with ends cut in V. Tack one bow to duck's neck and one each to top sleeve cuffs.

Fig. 5-10

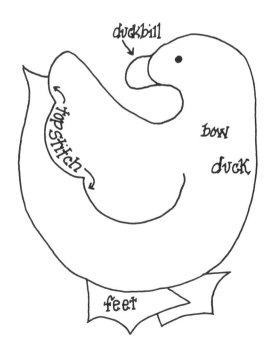

Just Ducky Sweater
Applique-Autumn

Presto Pizzazz

A Crested View Sweater

(See Figure 5-9)

Materials

White cardigan sweater

5 navy blue with gold anchor buttons, 1/2" diameter

Heat set crest appliqué

1 yard navy blue mini-rickrack

Red embroidery floss

Navy thread

Directions

1. Remove original buttons from sweater and replace with anchor buttons.

2. Fuse crest to upper left front of sweater following manufacturer's instructions. Hand stitch around crest to secure appliqué.

3. Stitch navy mini-rickrack around bottom of neckline ribbing with three strands red embroidery floss, using couching stitch. In same manner, trim around sweater cuff where ribbing meets sleeve, stretching slightly as you stitch.

6. *Wild About Winter*

When the holidays approach, a magical feeling touches us all, whether we are four, forty, or eighty-four. As we scurry about trying to fit a month's worth of errands into a week's time, it's important to make every moment count. It's also important to take time to make an outfit so special it brings not only joy to a child's holiday, but a wealth of memories, too.

The outfits in this chapter designed for Christmas holidays take the issue of limited time versus precious memories into consideration—with charming results. The appliquéd tabards can be buttoned on simple jumpers and shortalls to add that special holiday sparkle to tailored attire. The matching navy velveteen stocking completes the ensemble.

If making these outfits for a young toddler, sew on buttons with dental floss for most secure attachment. If you feel your fabric might tear if buttons are pulled, fuse some stiff iron-on interfacing to wrong side of fabric before buttons are sewn on for better results.

Directions are included for tabards for boys and girls, a matching Christmas stocking, appliqués for thermal undies, and a sweet bunny.

Fig. 6-1

♥ *Holiday Ensemble*
Jumper with Tabard
Shortall with Tabard
Stocking

♥ *Thermal Undies*
Skibear Undies
Bunny Undies

♥ *Bunny Toy*

♥ Twas the Night Before...
Holiday Ensemble

Girl's Velveteen Jumper with Tabard

(See Color Pages)

Fig. 6-2

Materials

Navy blue velveteen A-line dress or jumper
  with blouse

1/3 yard red quilted fabric

1/3 yard red mini-dot fabric (for lining)

2 yards 1/8" green dot grosgrain ribbon

1-1/2 yards each 1/8" red dot grosgrain
  ribbon and 1/8" white satin ribbon

1-1/2 yards 3/4" white gathered eyelet lace

3-mm red pompom

Scraps of:
  navy, green, and brown mini-dot fabrics
  lightweight iron-on interfacing
  fusible webbing

2 white 3/4" heart buttons

5 gold 10-mm star sequins

2 brass 3/8" jingle bells

6 assorted toy buttons: doll, clown face,
  snow queen, ballet slippers, kitty on
  skate board, and teddy bear

Gold metallic thread

Tissue paper

Matching threads

Directions

1. In order to fit the pattern in the book, I folded over the shoulder seam. Cut one each girl's tabard (Figure 6-4) from red quilted fabric and red mini-dot fabric (for lining).

2. Back mini-dot scraps with lightweight iron-on interfacing. Cut one sleigh from navy mini-dot and two reindeers from brown mini-dot (see Figure 6-3). Cut four ears from green mini-dot fabric. Position and fuse appliqué across tabard as shown in Figure 6-2; appliqué design using narrow-width satin stitch and matching threads. Topstitch detail on sleigh with red thread and a straight stitch.

3. Embroider antlers using doubled metallic gold thread with straight stitch. Embroider mouth with red thread and eye with navy thread, as shown in Figure 6-3.

4. Cut 18" piece of 1/8" green dot grosgrain ribbon. Starting at your far right reindeer, tack ribbon end at neck x on pattern. Twist ribbon and tack in place to hold every 2", tack at second reindeer's neck, and continue in same manner to sleigh. Tie small bow and tack to sleigh as shown in Figure 6-2.

5. Cut small red pompom in half and securely stitch for reindeer noses. Tack jingle bells at each reindeer's neck. Arrange toy buttons in sleigh for presents and sew in place. Stitch star sequins in sky with metallic gold thread as shown in Figure 6-2.

6. Right sides together, stitch eyelet lace around perimeter of tabard. With right sides together, pin appliquéd front to red mini-dot lining. Using 3/8" seam allowance, stitch around tabard, leaving 3" opening for turning. Clip corners and curves, turn right side out, and slip stitch opening closed.

7. Make buttonholes as indicated on the tabard pattern. Cut green dot grosgrain, red dot grosgrain, and white satin ribbon into 3/4-yard pieces. Hold ribbons together as if one piece and fold in half. Tack ribbons at center point to jumper side seam 1" below armhole. Repeat for other side.

8. Replace buttons on purchased jumper with heart buttons. (On dress, sew heart buttons 1" below shoulder seam.) Button tabard to jumper at shoulders. Thread ribbons through side buttonholes and tie into bows.

Fig. 6-3

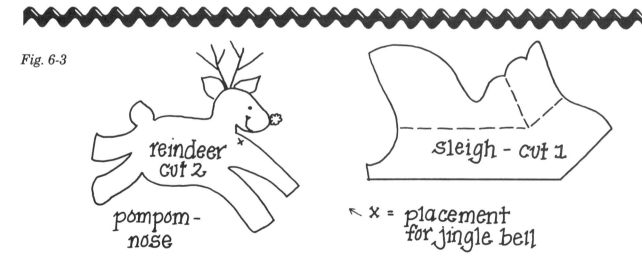

♥ **Laundering tip:** Place tabard in pillowcase and tie case shut. Wash on gentle cycle, remove from pillowcase, smooth tabard on flat surface, and hang to dry. Lightly press with cool iron, being careful not to iron the star sequins, as they can curl when exposed to excessive heat.

Fig. 6-4

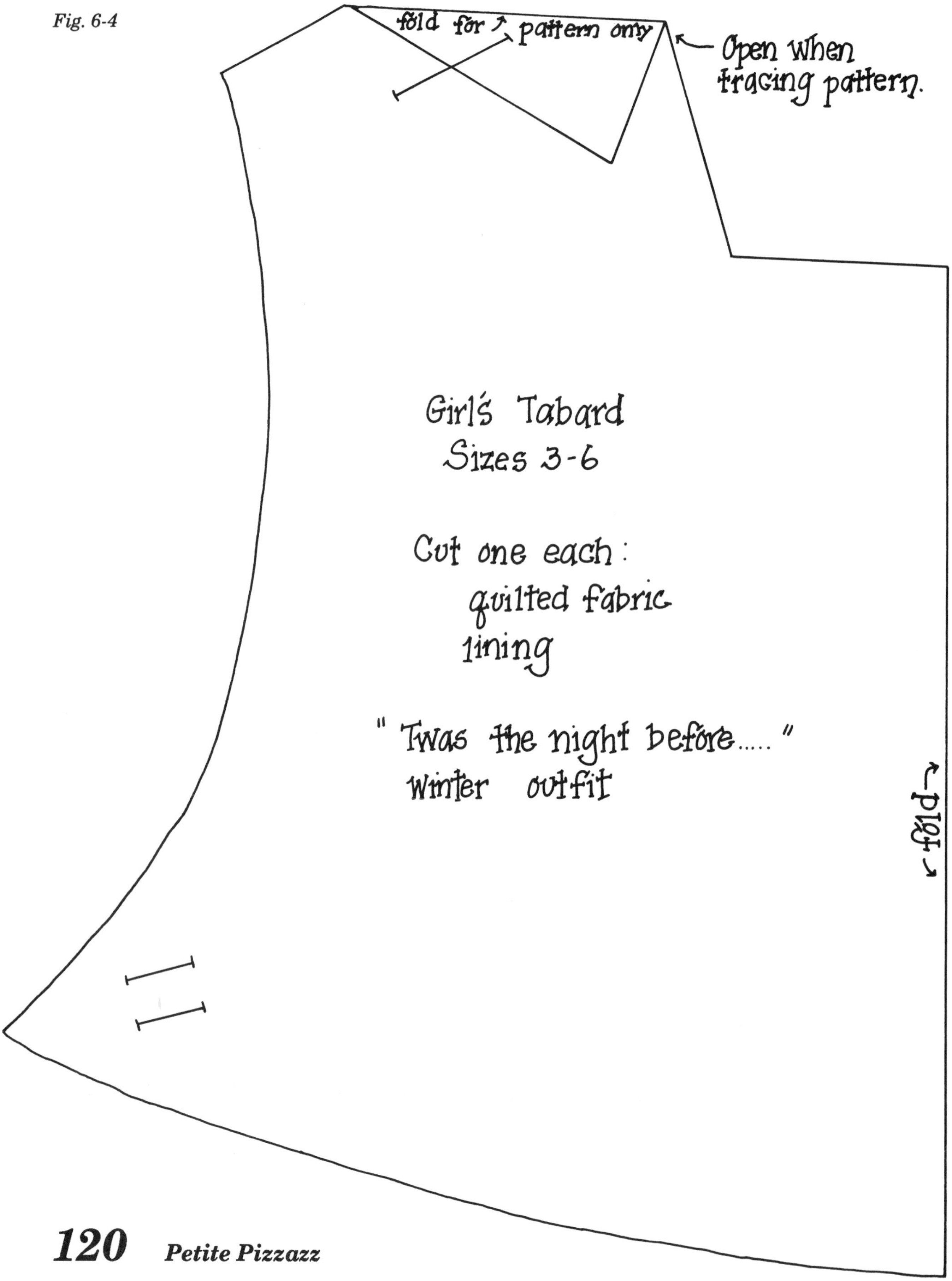

fold for → pattern only

Open when
tracing pattern.

Girl's Tabard
Sizes 3-6

Cut one each:
   quilted fabric
   lining

" 'Twas the night before....."
Winter outfit

← fold →

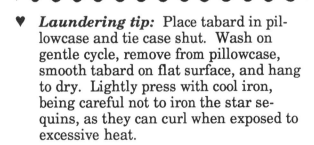

Boy's Velveteen Shortall with Tabard

(See Figure 6-1 and Color Pages)

Materials

Navy blue velveteen shortall with shirt
1/3 yard green quilted fabric
1/3 yard red mini-dot fabric (for lining)
Package red piping (1-1/2 yards needed)
1/2 yard 1/8" red dot ribbon
3-mm red pompom
Scraps of:
> navy, red, and brown mini-dot fabrics
> lightweight iron-on interfacing
> fusible webbing

4 red 1" star buttons
5 gold 10-mm star sequins
2 brass 3/8" jingle bells
6 novelty toy buttons: red airplane, red train, yellow horse, white duck, teddy bear, and Scottie dog
Gold metallic thread
Tissue paper
Matching threads

Directions

1. In order to fit the pattern in the book, I folded over the shoulder seam. Cut one each of boy's tabard (Figure 6-5) from green quilted fabric and red mini-dot fabric (for lining).

2. Follow Steps 2 through 5 for appliqué and trim detail in Girl's Velveteen Jumper directions. Note that for contrast the ears are red mini-dot rather than green; ribbon streamer from reindeers to sleigh is 1/8" red dot ribbon.

3. Stitch red piping around perimeter of tabard. With right sides together, pin appliquéd front to red mini-dot lining. Using 3/8" seam allowance, stitch around tabard, leaving 3" opening for turning. Clip corners and curves, turn right side out, and slip stitch opening closed.

4. Make buttonholes as indicated on the tabard pattern. Note that shoulder buttonhole falls on folded over portion of pattern. Replace shortall buttons with star buttons. Tack 1" red star buttons at side seams of shortall 1" below armholes. Button tabard to shortall at shoulders and sides.

♥ *Laundering tip:* Place tabard in pillowcase and tie case shut. Wash on gentle cycle, remove from pillowcase, smooth tabard on flat surface, and hang to dry. Lightly press with cool iron, being careful not to iron the star sequins, as they can curl when exposed to excessive heat.

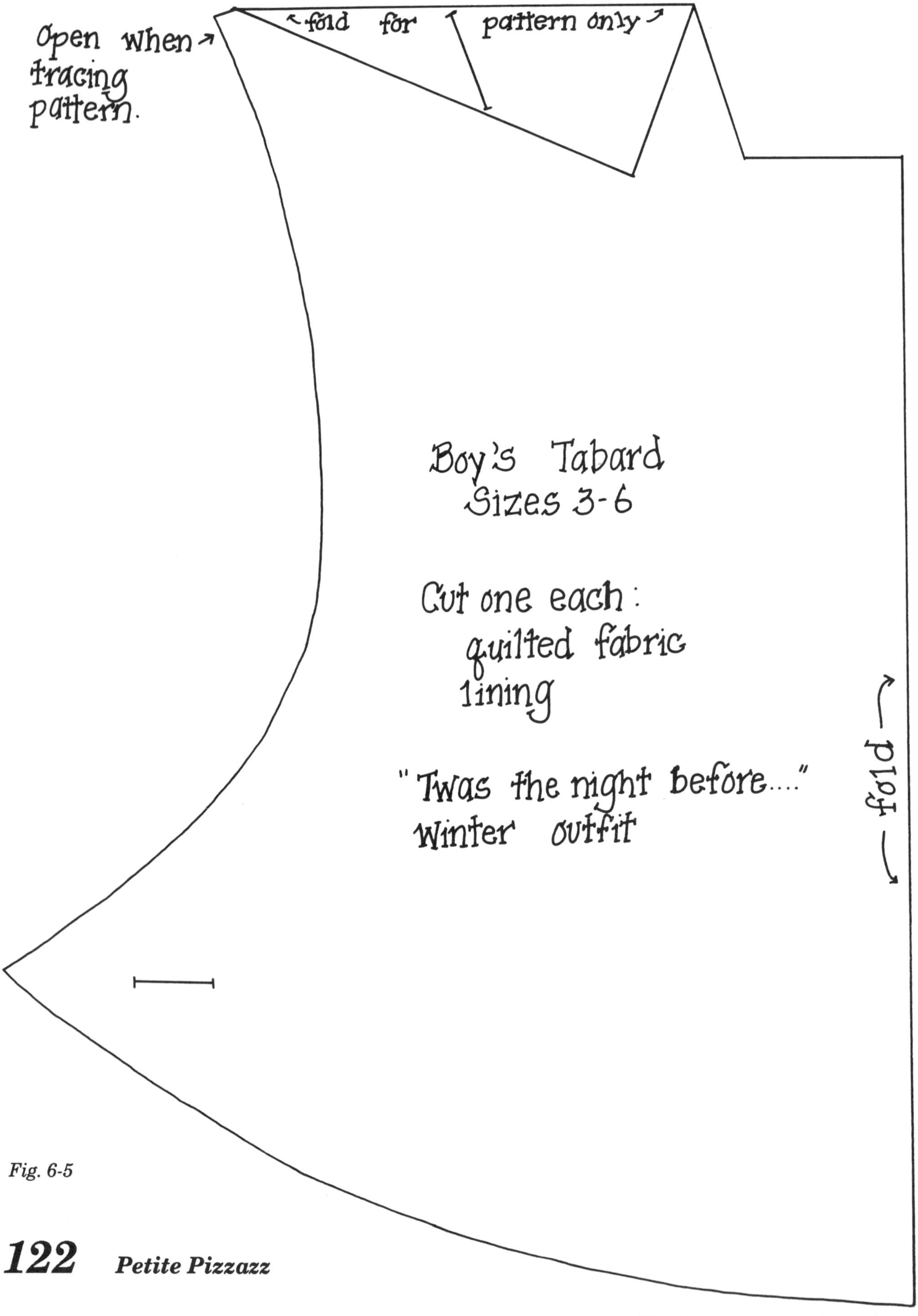

Open when →
tracing
pattern.

fold for   pattern only

Boy's Tabard
Sizes 3-6

Cut one each :
   quilted fabric
   lining

"Twas the night before...."
Winter outfit

← fold →

Fig. 6-5

Christmas Stocking

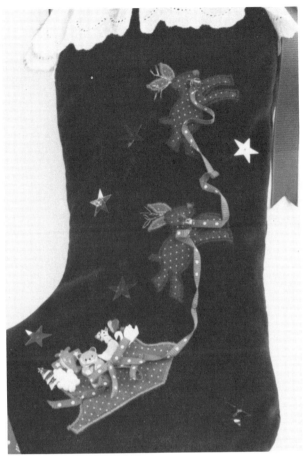

Fig. 6-6

♥ *Note:* Be sure to use a press cloth when ironing on velveteen.

♥ *Note:* Due to the trims used on these projects, sew buttons using dental floss or elastic thread to add extra strength to button attachments.

Materials

1/2 yard navy blue velveteen (will make two stockings)

1/4 yard 2" white gathered eyelet lace

1/4 yard 1" red plaid ribbon

1/2 yard red wide single fold bias tape

3/4 yard 1/2" red grosgrain ribbon

1/2 yard each: 1/8" green dot grosgrain and 1/8" white satin ribbons

1 yard 1/8" red dot grosgrain ribbon

3-mm red pompom

6 gold 10-mm star sequins

2 brass 3/8" jingle bells

2 brass bells

Santa Claus face button (for bow at top)

7 novelty holiday/toy buttons: teddy bear, Christmas tree, red airplane, white snowman, duck, swan, and red heart

Scraps of:

    green, red, and brown mini-dot fabrics

    3 coordinating red mini-print fabrics

    lightweight iron-on interfacing

    fusible webbing

    3/8" Christmas bow print ribbon

Gold metallic thread

Aleene's Tacky glue

Tissue paper

Press cloth

Matching threads

Dental floss

Directions

1. Trace pattern (Figures 6-7 and 6-8). Cut two navy blue velveteen stockings (one in reverse). Cut one 1-1/2" x 5" strip from each of three red mini-print fabrics. Arrange strips in pleasing pattern. Starting at guideline marked on pattern and with right sides together, pin first strip, right sides together, to velveteen stocking as indicated in Figure 6-8. Stitch 1/4" from left side of strip. Flip sewn strip right side up and press. Continue strip piecing stocking toe in this manner. Press. Trim excess fabric to match stocking outline.

Fig. 6-7

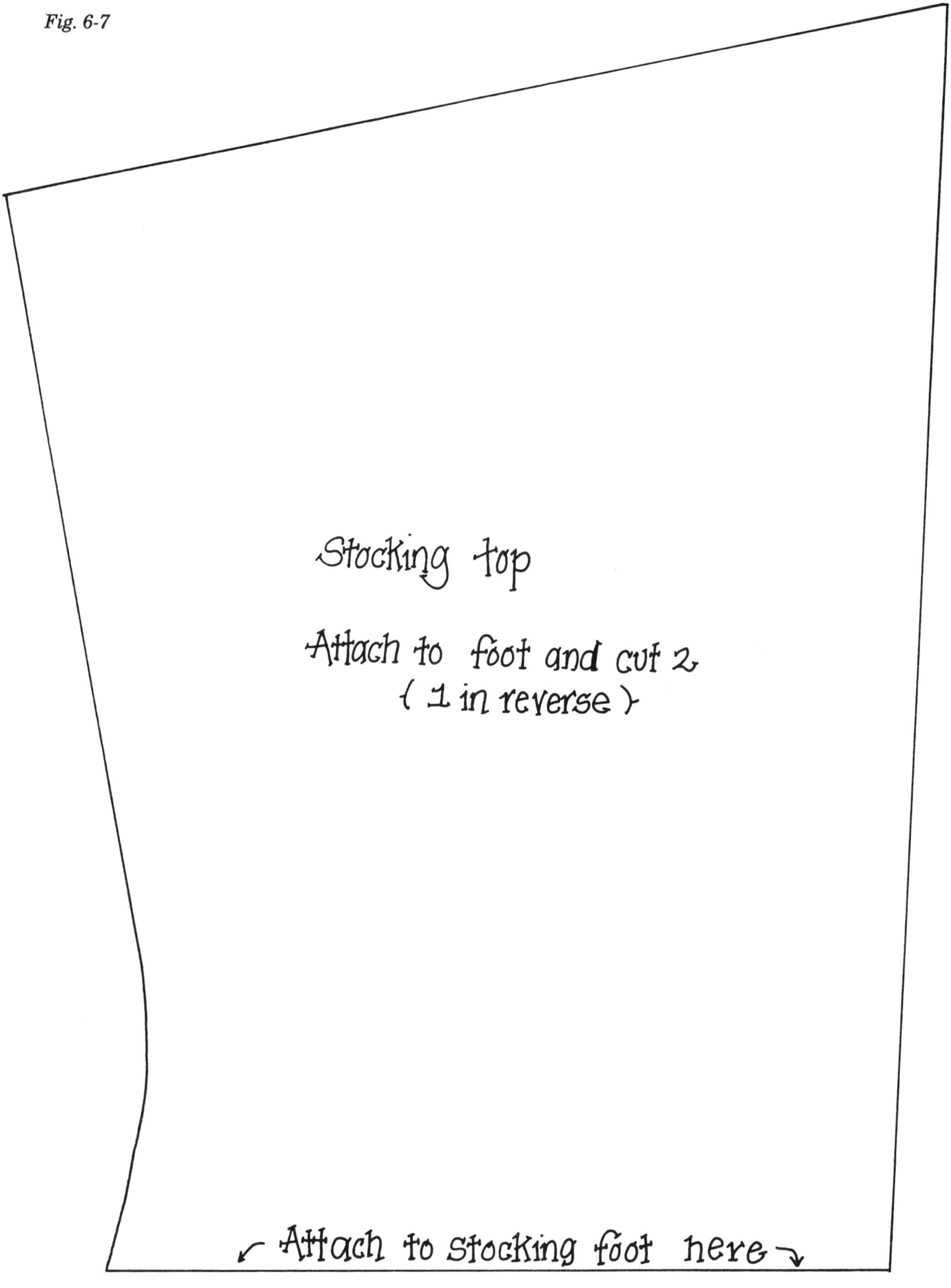

Stocking top

Attach to foot and cut 2
(1 in reverse)

⌐ Attach to stocking foot here ⌐

Fig. 6-8

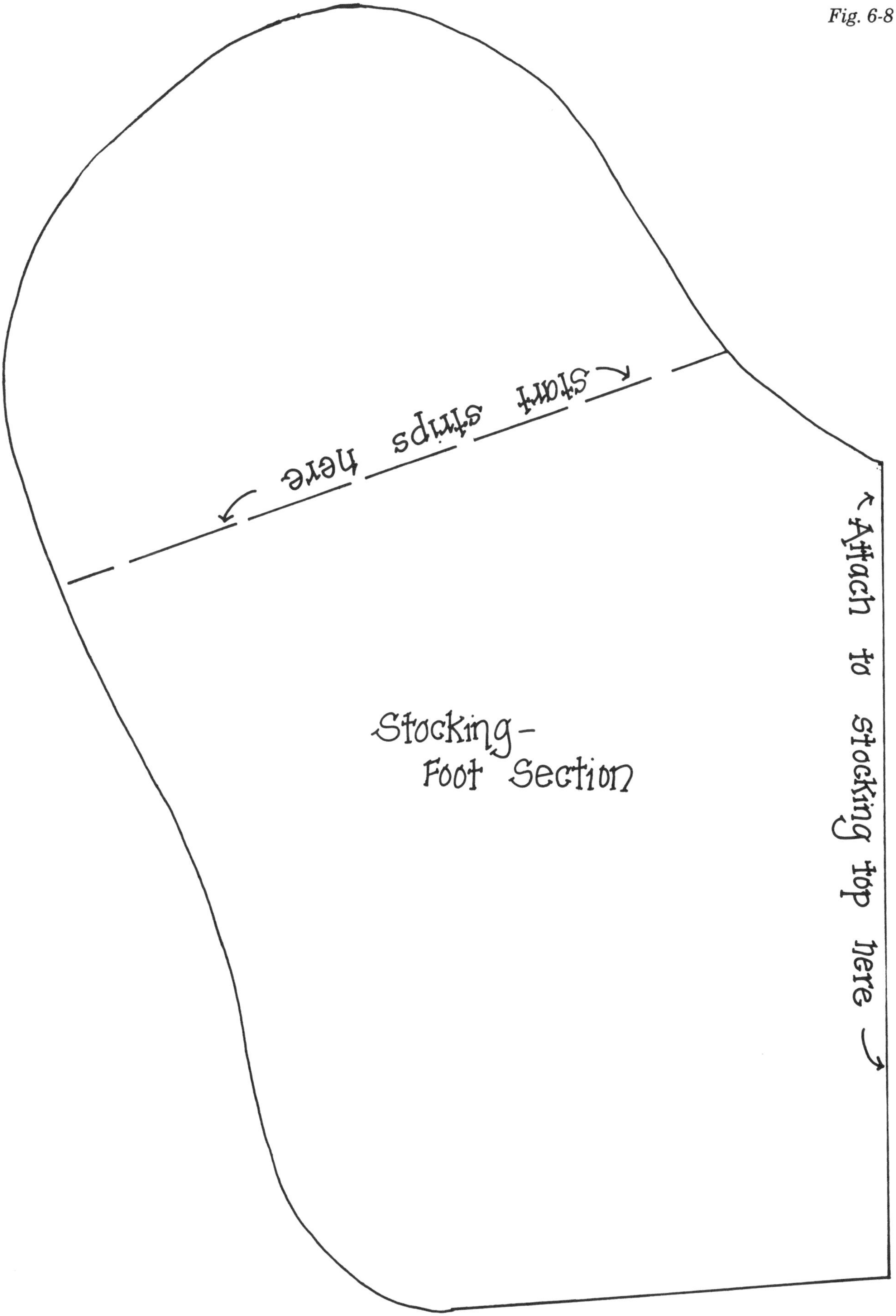

Start strips here →

← Attach to stocking top here →

Stocking-
Foot Section

2. Sew eyelet lace 2-1/4" from top of stocking. Using a narrow zigzag, stitch plaid ribbon above eyelet, so bottom edge of ribbon covers bias binding of eyelet lace.

3. Follow Steps 2 – 5 from girl's outfit directions for appliqué. The sleigh is cut from green mini-dot fabric. Note placement of appliqué with reindeer going up the stocking as shown in Figure 6-6. Ribbon streamer from reindeer to sleigh is 18" piece of 1/8" red dot grosgrain ribbon.

4. With right sides together, pin and stitch around stocking, leaving open at top. Clip curves and turn right side out. Right sides together, sew top edge with red single fold bias tape. Turn to inside and hand sew in place.

5. Make a four-loop bow using 1/2" red grosgrain ribbon and tack in center. Make two-loop bow using 1/8" ribbons and tack in center to center of red grosgrain bow. Glue Santa face button to center of bow. Tie brass bells to ends of green dot grosgrain ribbon. Tack decorated bow to heel side of stocking at top edge along seam. Fold Christmas bow print ribbon into loop and tack to inside seam of stocking above bow for hanger.

♥ *Thermal Undies*

When your little ones come inside chilled from a frosty day of building a snowman or skiing down favorite hills, have them slip into some toasty thermal undies, decorated with your own brand of personal style. The thermalwear items shown here use a variety of appliqué, lace, ribbon, buttons, rick-rack, and Slick paint to create "cute as a bunny" or sassy skibear undies. Think of these undies as blank white canvas, waiting to be appliquéd, trimmed, or painted to your heart's desire. Keep in mind that you can trim thermals in the same ways you would embellish today's popular jogging suits.

Skibear Thermals

(See Color Pages)

♥ *Laundering tip:* Pretreat all stains as soon as possible. Turn wrong side out and launder on gentle cycle in cold or warm water. Remove from washer, turn right side out, and lie flat to dry. Do not iron, as paint can melt!

Fig. 6-9

Materials

Pair of white thermal underwear (top and
  bottom)
Scraps of:
  forest green mini-print fabric
  red mini-dot fabric
  green mini-dot fabric
  black mini-dot fabric
  white piqué
  brown acrylic felt or knit fabric
  fusible webbing
1 yard lightweight iron-on interfacing
1/4 yard 1/8" green dot grosgrain ribbon
1/2 yard navy blue mini-rickrack
2 yards red medium-width rickrack
5-mm green pompom
2 red 1/2" round flat buttons (for ends of ski
  poles)
Embroidery floss in black, red, and white
Bottle white Tulip Slick paint
Prisma Glitter
Matching threads

Directions

1. Prewash thermal undies in hot water.
All fabric scraps should also be prewashed,
along with rickracks. Press fabric scraps
and rickracks with spray starch.

2. Cut a piece of lightweight iron-on interfacing to fit thermal top front piece and fuse
to wrong side of top front. Back all scraps to
be used for appliqué with lightweight iron-
on interfacing, and cut out as follows (see
Figure 6-10):

  cap cuff, white piqué
  cap, arm, sweater and tongue, red mini-
    dot fabric
  face, paw, and hind section, brown
    acrylic felt
  ski boots and nose, black mini-dot fabric
  two skis and one small tree, green mini-
    dot fabric
  one each large and one small tree, forest
    green mini-print

3. Cut small pieces of fusible webbing and
sandwich behind large tree appliqué piece.

Fuse large tree to right side of top, so armhole meets tree. Trim tree along armhole as
shown in Figure 6-9. Appliqué tree with medium-width satin stitch and matching
thread. Following pattern guideline, pin and
stitch navy rickrack from tree trunk across
and down front to make a ski hill, ending
about 1-1/2" above bottom edge at side.

4. Using fusible webbing between appliqués
and top, fuse appliqué scene in place. For
ski poles, cut 1/8" green dot grosgrain ribbon
into two 4-1/2" pieces and thread red buttons
on end of each ribbon for ski pole "basket."
Cut small strip of fusible webbing and place
under green dot ribbon. Position poles as
shown in Figure 6-10 and fuse to hold in
place. *Note:* The ribbon ski poles are
positioned under some pieces, **so layer
carefully.** Appliqué remaining pieces of
skibear with matching or contrasting
threads and narrow-width satin stitch.
Satin stitch topstitching detail shown by
dotted lines on pattern, using a narrow
width.

5. Using two strands of embroidery floss,
embroider face with satin stitch: eye, black;
freckles, black; and inner ears, red. Embroider a snowflake on sweater front with white
floss (or pearl cotton). Add buckle detail to
ski boots with white floss and lazy daisy
stitch. Hand stitch ski poles in place. Tack
green pompom to top of ski cap.

6. Trim neckline, wrist cuffs, and bottom
edge of top with red rickrack. At neckline
and wrist, position rickrack at the edge of
ribbing, and stretch as you straight stitch.
This stretching enables garment to expand
during dressing and undressing.

7. Fuse two small trees to upper left leg of
thermal bottoms. Cut piece of lightweight
iron-on interfacing slightly larger than
appliqués and fuse to **wrong** side of leg
under fused tree appliqués. Appliqué trees
with narrow-width satin stitch and matching
threads. Trim ankle cuffs with red rickrack,
stretching as you did for wrists and neckline
in Step 6. *Note:* In order to trim wrists and
ankles, you need a free-arm sewing machine.
If your machine does not have this feature,
attach rickrack by hand, following above
instructions.

Fig. 6-10

8. Trim away excess interfacing from wrong side of appliqués. Dot scene with white Slick paint for falling snow and sprinkle with glitter. Allow paint to dry thoroughly.

cut here for small tree→

←fold↴

Skibear Appliqués
for Thermal Undies
- winter -

rickrack

Note: This is an
intricate appliqué
design - work
slowly and build
the design for
best results!

"Cute as a Bunny" Thermals

Fig. 6-11

Materials

Pair of white thermal underwear (top and bottom)

2 yards 1" white ruffled cluny lace

3 yards 3/8" white with pink heart print ribbon

3 yards 1/8" pink dot grosgrain ribbon

1 yard 1/16" white satin ribbon

3 pink 5/8" pompoms

5 white "bunny with pink flowers" buttons

Scraps of:
  pink mini-heart print fabric
  light blue mini-floral print fabric
  white floral mini-print fabric
  fusible webbing

1/2 yard lightweight iron-on interfacing

Embroidery floss in pink and light blue

Disappearing ink marking pen

Matching threads

Directions

1. Prewash thermal undies in hot water. All fabric scraps for appliqué should also be prewashed, along with cluny lace. Press fabric scraps and cluny lace with spray starch.

2. Back all fabric scraps listed with lightweight iron-on interfacing and cut out the appliqués as follows (see Figure 6-12):

> three bunnies (one in reverse) and one small heart, pink mini-heart print fabric
> one large heart, light blue print
> one small heart, white floral print

Draw topstitching details and face on bunnies using disappearing ink marking pen.

3. Position and fuse appliqués to top front with bunnies facing each other, slightly overlapping at edges of large light blue heart. Cut a piece of lightweight iron-on interfacing larger than appliqué scene and fuse to wrong side of top front, under appliqué scene. Tuck small pieces of fusible web under appliqué pieces. Appliqué hearts and bunnies (including topstitching) with matching threads and medium-width satin stitch.

4. Tack pink pompoms in place for fluffy tails. Embroider pink nose and blue eye with two strands of embroidery floss and satin stitch. Tie two small four-loop bows from 1/16" white satin ribbon and tack at each bunny's neck at X.

5. Fuse small pink mini-heart print heart to left upper sleeve. Cut piece of lightweight iron-on interfacing larger than heart and fuse to wrong side of sleeve. With matching thread, appliqué heart to sleeve with narrow-width satin stitch.

6. Using a narrow zigzag, trim neckline, wrist cuffs, and bottom edge with white cluny lace. Stretch knit as you attach lace so garment can stretch as needed during dressing and undressing.

7. Position and fuse bunny to right upper leg of thermal bottoms. (Back appliqué area on wrong side of thermal bottoms with lightweight iron-on interfacing as above.) Appliqué bunny with matching threads and medium-width satin stitch, trimming bunny with embroidery, pompom, and bow, as in Step 4. ***Note:*** In order to trim wrists and ankles, you need a free-arm sewing machine. If your machine does not have this feature, attach lace and rickrack trims by hand following above instructions.

8. Cut 1-yard pieces of 3/8" white heart print ribbon and 1/8" pink dot grosgrain ribbon. Make six-loop bow with heart print ribbon and tack in center. Make six-loop bow with pink dot ribbon and tack through center to center of heart ribbon bow. Fan out ribbon loops. Tack bunny button to center of bow. Stitch fancy bow to upper right side of ribbing at neckline.

9. Cut remaining ribbons into four each 18" pieces. Make four four-loop bows as in Step 8 with bunny buttons in center. Tack fancy bows at outer wrist and ankle cuffs.

Fig. 6-12

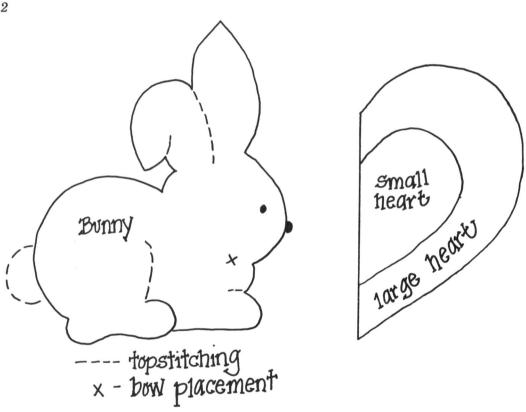

---- topstitching
× - bow placement

"Cute As A Bunny" Appliqués

♥ *Presto Pizzazz—Honey Bunny*

Fig. 6-13

This project was designed with two thoughts in mind: to create a cuddly friend reminiscent of the past, and to design a toy that would be ideal for tucking in with a child at night. Scrap bag trims make this project one that will be treasured and loved. Bunny can be sewn in an hour; add another hour for the dress. When making bunny for child under 3, omit buttons for eyes and embroider eyes using satin stitch. Omit buttons on bunny dress.

Materials

1/3 yard cream-colored sherpa fleece (will make two bunnies)

1/2 yard cream and pink heart mini-print fabric

2 brown 3/8" half-round buttons

Large white bunny button

Pink 1/4" heart button

1 yard 1/2" off-white flat heart lace trim

1/2 yard 5/8" blue grosgrain picot ribbon

1-1/2 yard 3/8" white with pink heart print ribbon

1 yard 1/8" pink dot grosgrain ribbon

1/4 yard 3/4" off-white ruffled eyelet lace trim

Pink 1/2" pompom

Polyfil stuffing

Disappearing ink marking pen

Aleene's Tacky glue

Dental floss

Matching threads

Directions:

Note: Please use 1/4" seam allowance unless otherwise indicated.

1. Transfer patterns (Figures 6-14 through 6-18) for front body piece, back body piece, and ears to 20 lb. bond paper (typing weight). In order to fit the patterns in the book, I had to split up the patterns. When drafting your patterns, attach bunny heads as shown on pattern pieces. Cut out paper patterns, including ovals. Using disappearing ink marking pen, trace around patterns and cut-out ovals on wrong side of sherpa. Trace around oval darts. Mark all triangular darts. Cut out one back piece, two front pieces (one in reverse), and two ears (one in reverse) from sherpa fleece. For best results, cut from wrong side of fleece. Cut two ears (one in reverse) from the heart print fabric.

2. With right sides together, pin sherpa ear and lining ear together, tucking fleece inwards. Stitch around ear, leaving open as shown in Figure 6-18. Repeat for other ear. Clip top corner and turn right side out. Set aside.

3. With right sides together, pin and stitch center front body seam. Stitch all darts on both front and back pieces and trim away excess fabric. Lining side of ear against right side of head, baste ears to front piece, lightly pinching them to make a pleat, centering each ear by each side's top dart. With right sides together, pin back to front, tucking fleece inwards. Stitch around bunny, leaving open at bottom. Reinforce stitching at neck and around arm and leg curves. Clip curves, turn right side out, and stuff firmly. Hand stitch closed.

4. Securely stitch brown buttons in place for eyes. *Optional:* Use dental floss when stitching eyes for sturdy attachment. Glue or tack pink pompom in place for nose.

5. To make dress, from heart print fabric, cut skirt 12" x 22", two sleeves (one in reverse), two back bodice pieces (one in reverse) and one front bodice (see Figures 6-19 and 6-20). With right sides together, stitch shoulder seams.

6. Gather sleeve caps, adjust to fit armholes, and stitch in place. Turn under cuffs 1/8" and trim cuff edges with flat heart lace trim. With right sides together, stitch underarm seams. Fold under neckline edge 1/8" and stitch. Fold under center back openings 1/8" and hem. Press completed top.

7. Hem skirt along 22" edge and trim with flat heart lace. Stitch two 1/4" tucks along skirt bottom. Stitch center back seam, leaving 6" opening at top. Gather raw edge, pin, adjust gathers evenly, and stitch skirt to bodice. Fit dress on bunny. Hand stitch back opening closed. Hand stitch a row of running stitches 1/2" from fabric cuff edge of sleeves, pull to gather, and knot securely. Poof sleeves for a Victorian look. Tie 1/8" pink dot grosgrain ribbon around wrists over gathering stitches into a bow.

8. Starting at center back, tack ruffled eyelet lace trim around neckline, tucking under and securing lace end at center back. Tie four-loop bow of white with pink heart ribbon.

9. Tie 5/8" blue grosgrain picot ribbon around waist with bow in back, cutting ends in V. Tie bow using 3/8" white with pink heart print ribbon, cut ends at angle, and glue to left ear with 1/4" pink heart button in center of bow.

10. Tie six-loop bows of white with pink heart ribbon and pink dot grosgrain ribbon. Tack bows together with bunny button in center of bow. Stitch fancy bow to left side of ribbon waistband.

Fig. 6-14

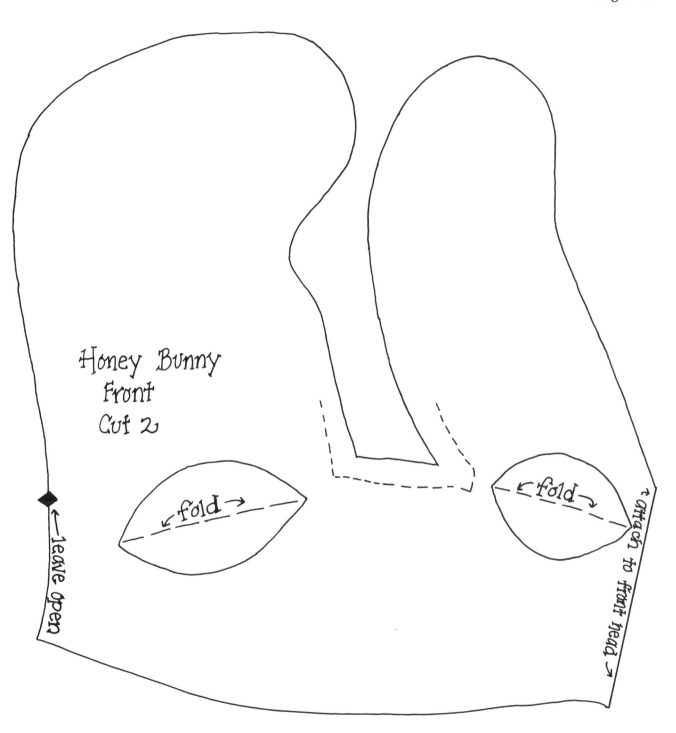

Honey Bunny
Front
Cut 2

← fold →

← fold →

← leave open

↗ attach to front head ↗

Fig. 6-15

← attach to head back here ↗

Honey Bunny Back.
Cut 1

← fold →

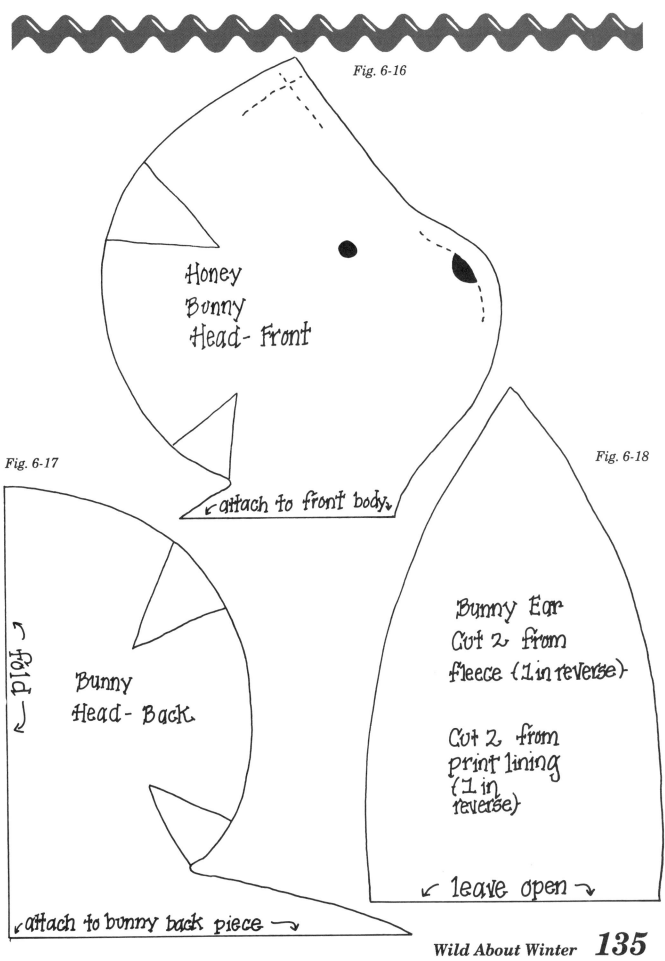

Fig. 6-16

Honey
Bunny
Head- Front

⤿ attach to front body⤸

Fig. 6-17

⤿ fold ⤸

Bunny
Head- Back

⤿ attach to bunny back piece ⤸

Fig. 6-18

Bunny Ear
Cut 2 from
fleece (1 in reverse)

Cut 2 from
print lining
(1 in
reverse)

⤿ leave open ⤸

Fig. 6-19

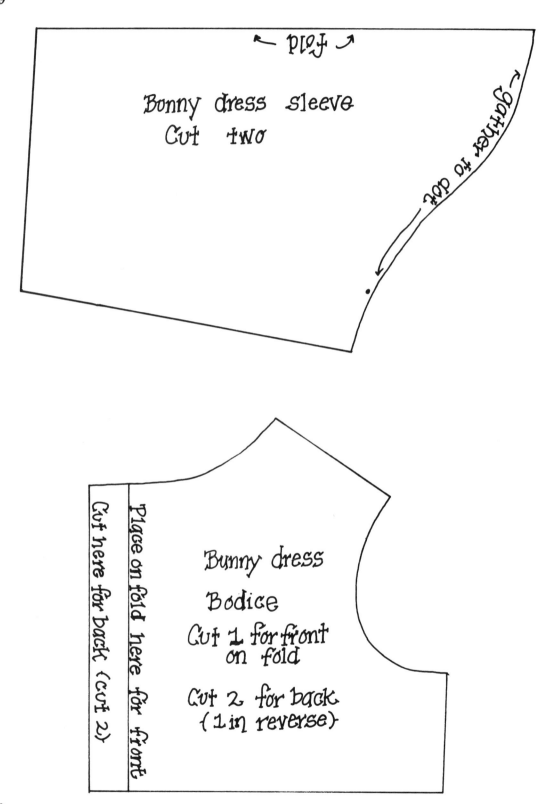

Bunny dress sleeve
Cut two

← fold →

~gather to dot

Bunny dress

Bodice

Cut 1 for front
on fold

Cut 2 for back
(1 in reverse)

Place on fold here for front

Cut here for back (cut 2)

Fig. 6-20

♥ *A Final Word*

Sewing for babies and children taps into your treasure chest of memories, allowing you to recapture some of your childhood joys. Remember your first tricycle, first birthday party, first day in school? You can translate those cherished memories into appliqués to embellish an outfit for your child.

Taking the time to give a part of yourself in a special outfit, costume, or fancy patch on a loved pair of jeans is another way to say "I love you" to your children. In addition you'll feel a wonderful sense of accomplishment: the garment, accessory, or proj-ect is proof of your creative talents. When you sew for a child, the rewards are tenfold: you are giving them a hug to wear all day.

There is another special aspect of sewing I love: sharing. If you need help with a sewing problem, are looking for a particular mail order source, or would like to share an idea, don't hesitate to write. Over the years, I've developed a network of creative stitchers who have become long-distance, treasured friends. I welcome letters and notes and will do my best to answer as quickly as possible.

Happy stitching!

♥ **Barb Griffin**
2843 Trenton Way
Ft. Collins, CO 80526

Resource List

♥ Periodicals

Featuring children's wear ideas and projects

Child Magazine
110 Fifth Avenue
New York, NY 10011
Bimonthly; $9.97 subscription

Country Handcrafts Magazine
5400 South Sixth Street
Greendale, WI 53129
Bimonthly; $13.95 subscription

Creative Classics for Kids
Newsletter
2843 Trenton Way
Ft. Collins, CO 80526
Published 5 times a year
Send LSASE for information

Creative Ideas for Living
Magazine
810 Seventh Avenue
New York, NY 10019
Bimonthly; $15.97 subscription

Creative Needle Magazine
1500 Jupiter Road
Lookout Mountain, GA 30750
Quarterly; $3.00 sample issue

Creative Sewing Magazine
1500 Jupiter Road
Lookout Mountain, GA 30750
Bimonthly; $3.00 sample issue

Family Circle Magazine
110 Fifth Avenue
New York, NY 10011
Published every three weeks;
$15.97 subscription

Kitty Benton Designletter with
Swatches
285 West Broadway, Suite 440
New York, NY 10013
Published five times a year;
$2.50 sample issue, $12.50
subscription

Jerry Stock's Stitching
Vignettes Newsletter
P.O. Box 2059
Beaufort, SC 29901
Bimonthly; $3.00 sample issue,
$12.00 subscription

Sew Beautiful Magazine
518 Madison Street
Huntsville, AL 35801
Published five times a year;
$5.00 sample issue, $23.00
subscription

Sew News
P.O. Box 1790
Peoria, IL 61656
Monthly; $15.97 subscription

Sewing Sampler—Business
Edition Newsletter
P.O. Box 39
Springfield, MN 56087
Quarterly; $4.00 sample issue,
$12.00 subscription

Sewing Sampler— Children's
Edition Newsletter
P.O. Box 39
Springfield, MN 56087
Bimonthly; $2.00 sample issue,
$10.00 subscription

Threads Magazine
63 Main Street
Newtown, CT 06407
Bimonthly; $3.95 sample issue,
$20 subscription

Update Sewing Newsletter
2269 Chestnut, Suite 269
San Francisco, CA 94123
Bimonthly; $18.00 subscription

Victoria Magazine
224 West 57th Street
New York, NY 10019
Monthly; $15.97 subscription

♥ Alternative Pattern Companies for Children's Wear

Ansley & Co.
Becky Tollison
341 North Ruby
Ruleville, MS 38771
(601) 756-2922
$1.00 catalog

Alpel Publishing
Leila Albala
P.O. Box 203
Chambly, Quebec
Canada J3L 4B3
(514) 658-6205
$1.00 sample pattern
and catalog

Angel Wears
Eunice Logan
120 Shaker Landing Road
Harrodsburg, KY 40330
(606) 734-5290
$2.00 catalog

Barb's Kids
Barb Griffin
2843 Trenton Way
Ft. Collins, CO 80526
(303) 223-0255
$1.00 catalog

Beaucoup, Inc.
P.O. Box 1266
Greenville, MS 38701
(601) 378-8868
$1.00 catalog

The Best Dressed, Inc.
105 Cheyenne Drive
Hendersonville, NC 37075
(615) 824-6680
$5.00 catalog

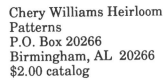

Chery Williams Heirloom
Patterns
P.O. Box 20266
Birmingham, AL 20266
$2.00 catalog

The Children's Corner
P.O. Box 150161
Nashville, TN 37215
(615) 292-1746
$1.00 catalog

The Clothesline
Jenny Wren Limited
7166 South Hudson Circle
Littleton, CO 80112
(303) 773-0364
$1.00 catalog

Creative Keepsakes
P.O. Box 5067
Garland, TX 75047-5067
$1.00 brochure

Deborah's Designs
144 Honeysuckle Drive
Hendersonville, TN 37075
(615) 824-6977
$2.00 brochure

Ginger Designs
Box 3241
Newport Beach, CA 92663
$1.00 catalog

Heirlooms Only!
10198 Warwick Boulevard
Newport News, VA 23601
(804) 599-8557

Homespun Treasures
2416 Stone Creek
Plano, TX 75075
(214) 964-3324
$1.00 brochure

J. Vehr Designs
6510 Darby Way
Spring, TX 77389
(713) 376-1765
$2.00 brochure

Kwik-Sew Pattern Co.
3000 Washington Avenue
North
Minneapolis, MN 55411
(612) 521-7651
$3.50 catalog

Maggie's Classics
P.O. Box 7103
Mobile, AL 36607
(205) 473-2970
Free brochure

Martha Pullen, Inc.
518 Madison Street
Huntsville, AL 35801
1-800-547-4176
$1.00 catalog

PBJK's Designs, Inc.
(Peanut Butter 'n Jelly Kids)
3607 Old Shell Road
Mobile, AL 36608
(205) 342-8017
$2.00 catalog

Prairie Clothing Co.
939 Dewey
Iowa City, IA 52245
(319) 354-0235
(319) 351-3490
Catalog $2.00

Sew Little Pattern Co.
P.O. Box 3613
Salem, OR 97302
(503) 371-3274
$1.00 catalog

Sewing Sampler Productions
P.O. Box 39
Springfield, MN 56087
(507) 723-5011
$1.00 catalog

Small Threads
P.O. Box 162137
Sacramento, CA 95816
Brochure available

Special Request
4117 Saunders Avenue
Nashville, TN 37216
(615) 262-5145
$2.00 catalog

Stretch-n-Sew, Inc.
P.O. Box 185
Eugene, OR 97440
Free brochure

Sunrise Designs
Box 277
Orem, UT 84059
Free catalog

Victoria's Originals
P.O. Box 691182
Houston, TX 77269
(713) 893-2017
$1.00 catalog + $3.00 for
swatches

Yvonne Denise Designs
P.O. Box 980911
Houston, TX 77098
(713) 529-2430
$5.00 catalog and swatches

A Work of Heart
P.O. Box 1355
Grass Valley, CA 95945
(916) 272-LACE

♥ Mail-Order Fabric Sources

Britex-by-Mail
146 Geary
San Francisco, CA 94108
(415) 392-2910
Send LSASE and requests for
samples

Calico House
Route 4
Box 16-M
Scottsville, VA 24590
$2.00 catalog

Carolina Mills Factory Outlet
Box V
Hwy 76 West
Branson, MO 65616
(417) 334-2291
Sample swatches $2.00

Cottons, Etc.
228 Genessee Street
Oneida, NY 13421
(315) 363-6834
$1.00 + LSASE for swatches

Daisy Kingdom
134 NW 8th
Portland, OR 97209
(503) 222-9033
$2.00 catalog

Denham Designs
P.O. Box 4
Jacksonville, NC 28541
1-800-451-7143
(919) 347-2436
$7.00 swatch portfolio

Fabrications Fabric Club
Box 2162
South Vineland, NJ 08360
$10.00 annual membership
with quarterly mailings

G Street Fabrics
11854 Rockville Pike
Rockville, MD 20852
$10 sample charts

Little Legacies
P.O. Box 587
Pell City, AL 35125
1-800-451-1193
$5.00 catalog and swatches

Little Stitches
P.O. Box 76769
Atlanta, GA 30328
(404) 225-5949
$1.00 catalog

Linda's Silver Needle
32 Westmoreland
Naperville, IL 60540
$3.00 catalog

Martha Pullen, Inc.
518 Madison Street
Huntsville, AL 35801
1-800-547-4176
$1.00 catalog

Norway Fabric Outlet
P.O. Box 307
Norway, ME 04268
$2.00 current sample set

Oppenheim's
Department 414
North Manchester, IN 46962
(219) 982-6848
$2.00 catalog + swatches

Sew 'n Sew
c/o Vicki Mason
24025 SE Hwy 212
Boring, OR 97009
$3.00 current catalog and
swatches

Sew Natural-Fabrics by Mail
Route 1, Box 428-C
Middlesex, NC 27557
(919) 235-2754
$2.00 catalog and swatches

Sewing Sampler Productions
Designer Fabrics by Mail
P.O. Box 39
Springfield, MN 56087
(507) 723-5011
$1.00 catalog

The Smocking Bird
2904B Linden Avenue
Birmingham, AL 35209
(205) 879-7662
$4.00 catalog

Spechler-Vogel
234 West 39th Street
New York, NY 10018
1-800-223-2031
(212) 564-6177

The Stitching Post
161 Elm
P.O. Box 280
Sisters, OR 97759
$1.00 catalog

Yesterday's Stitches
P.O. Box 2781
Monterey, CA 93940
(408) 484-9601
$2.50 catalog

♥ Buttons

Please note: Button assortments for specific projects in
this book are available. Send
LSASE for listing and prices to:

Barb's Kids
2843 Trenton Way
Ft. Collins, CO 80526
(303) 223-0255

Albe Creations
2920 Century Square
Winston-Salem, NC 27106
(919) 924-2911

Beaucoup, Inc.
P.O. Box 1266
Greenville, MS 38701
(601) 378-8868
$1.00 catalog

Button Creations
3801 Stump Road
Doylestown, PA 18901
1-800-346-0233
$2.00 catalog

Buttons & Things Factory
Outlet Store
24 Main Street
Route 1
Freeport, ME 04032
(207) 865-4480

The Button Shop
P.O. Box 1065
Oak Park, IL 60304

Debra B. Rutherford
Handcrafted Ceramic Buttons
P.O. Box 100
Essex, MA 01929
(508) 768-6572

Dogwood Lane
RR5, Box 162A
Sullivan, IN 47882
$2.50 color catalog

The Hand Works
Box 386
Pecos, NM 87552
(505) 757-6730
$2.00 catalog

A Homespun Heart
810 Bluffwood Lane
Iowa City, IA 52245
(319) 351-3490

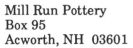

Mill Run Pottery
Box 95
Acworth, NH 03601

The Name Game
3324 Gray Moss Road
Matthews, NC 28105

Randy Miller Pewter Buttons
North Road
East Alstead, NH 03602

Renaissance Buttons
516 Dempster Street
Evanston, IL 60202
(312) 475-5262
Note: Minimum order $25

Sew Unique
Barbara Robertson
5656 Calyn Road
Catonsville, MD 21228
$1.00 catalog

Stella Buttons
University Station
P.O. Box 5632
Seattle, WA 98105

Windy Hill Creations
Handmade Stoneware Buttons
Route 1
Adams, TN 37010
(615) 696-2169

♥ Notions and Sewing Supplies

Aardvark Adventures
P.O. Box 2449
Livermore, CA 94550
$1.00 sample issue

Clotilde
1909 SW First Avenue
Ft. Lauderdale, FL 33315
(305) 761-8655

Creations by Jerry Stocks
P.O. Box 2059
Beaufort, SC 29901
(803) 524-6997

Creative Trims
18 Woodland Drive
Lincroft, NJ 07738

Custom Zips
P.O. Box 1200
South Norwalk, CT 06856

Donna Lee's Sewing Center
25234 Pacific Hwy South
Kent, WA 98032
(206) 941-9466
$3.00 catalog

The Fabric Carr
P.O. Box 1083
Los Altos, CA 94022
(415) 948-7373

Home-Sew
Bethlehem, PA 18018

Maryland Trims
P.O. Box 3508
Silver Spring, MD 20901
$1.75 catalog

Nancy's Notions, Ltd.
P.O. Box 683
Beaver Dam, WI 53916
(414) 887-0391

Newark Dressmaker Supply
P.O. Box 2448
Lehigh Valley, PA 18001
(215) 837-7500

The Perfect Notion
566 Hoyt Street
Darien, CT 06820
(203) 968-1257

Pioneer Specialty Products
Box 412
Holden, MA 01520
$1.00 catalog

Oppenheim's
Dept. 415
North Manchester, IN 46962
(219) 982-6848
$2.00 catalog with samples

SewCraft
P.O. Box 1869
Warsaw, IN 46580
(219) 269-4046

Sew Natural-Fabrics by Mail
Route 1, Box 428C
Middlesex, NC 27557
(919) 235-2754
$2.00 catalog and swatches

Sewing Emporium
1087 Third Avenue
Chula Vista, CA 92010
(619) 420-3490
$2.00 catalog

Sewing Sampler Productions
P.O. Box 39
Springfield, MN 56087
(507) 723-5011
$1.00 catalog

Speed Stitch
3113-D Broadpoint Drive
Harbor Heights, FL 33983
$3.00 catalog

Treadleart
25834 Narbonne Avenue, Suite I
Lomita, CA 90717
1-800-327-4222
$1.50 catalog

Index